The Italian Legacy in Washington, D.C.

Under the Patronage of the Italian Presidency
of the Council of Ministers

The Italian Legacy
in Washington, D.C.

Architecture, Design, Art and Culture

edited by Luca Molinari and Andrea Canepari

We wish to express our deepest gratitude
to the following for their generous contribution
to the publication of this volume:

When the Framers of the American Constitution constructed the legal foundations of our system of government, they sought to create something truly unique and distinctly American. Their efforts resulted in an exceptional form of government designed to protect the civil rights and civil liberties of its citizens above all else.

When our young nation searched for the architectural forms that would inspire our builders and house our government institutions, however, America looked to the masters of Europe, and particularly the Italians. As a result, styles and designs first conceived of by sons of Rome ages ago gave shape to many of the most visible and well-known structures in Washington, D.C.

From Jefferson's Monticello in Charlottesville, Virginia to the United States Capitol in our nation's seat of power, Italian influences abound. The beauty of Italian-influenced architecture pleases the eye and provides the blueprint for government buildings across our nation.

Even as our nation grew, and our Capitol itself expanded, Italian influences remained. Italian artisans, most notably Constantino Brumidi, decorated the interior of the relatively new wing that now houses the United States Senate, and painted the Rotunda's awe-inspiring fresco The Apotheosis of George Washington, honoring the father of our country. The Capitol's ornately adorned Brumidi Corridors remain the most immediately recognizable aspect of its interior and continue to impress visitors from around the world.

I take pride that the land of my ancestors also gave life to the remarkable designs that helped give shape to the United States Capitol, where, for the first time, an Italian-American serves as Speaker of the House. These facts are a testament to the splendor of America and a tribute to the beauty that Italian architects created and inspired.

Nancy Pelosi
Speaker of the House of Representatives

It is a pleasure and a privilege to preface this publication on the Italian influence in the architectural and cultural story of Washington, D.C. Admiring the Capital and its imposing monuments, we may rightly affirm that the friendship between the United States and Italy is "sculpted" in the very same symbols of the American democracy.

Washington, D.C. was actually conceived as a tribute to the Roman Republican Age. Its architectural design, straight and simple in its lines, but monumental and imperial in its shape, has succeeded in transporting into modernity and functionality the essence of Ancient Rome. The Federal Capital is a living example of neo-Classicism. A courageous step, taken at the very beginning of the nineteenth century, to modernize the European concept of the city in a new continent, preserving the style, but improving efficiency and anticipating the future.

As Italians, it was therefore quite natural to contribute to enhance the beauty of the United States' Federal Capital and the seat of its democratic institutions. Visiting the city and its landmarks it is easy to recognize these contributions and the "Italian imprints."

The book offers an accurate overview of this. Constantino Brumidi is one of the main contributors to the enrichment of the shape of the city. Known as the "American Michelangelo," he spent 25 years of his life decorating the Capitol interior dome. The Apotheosis of George Washington *in the Rotunda,* The Rising to Heaven of George Washington *and the six allegoric scenes that enrich the perimeter of the canopy are among his most important masterpieces. Brumidi is also the author of the paintings of the Speaker's Room and the designer of the Corridors that take his name. He brought the art of ancient Roman, Renaissance, and Baroque styles, symbols, and techniques of wall painting in the heart of Washington, D.C.*

Enrico Causici, Antonio Capellano, and Luigi Persico were the artists who visibly secured for ever the founding values of the American democracy in their mythological sculptures, in the same place where the legislators of the nation get together. Attilio Piccirilli and his five brothers carved the Memorial *of the sixteenth American President, Abraham Lincoln.*

The "Italian imprints" in Washington, D.C. can be also traced in the architecture of many public and private buildings, like the Jefferson Memorial, largely inspired by the genius and the artistic school of Andrea di Pietro della Gondola, known as Andrea Palladio. Next year, we will celebrate the fifth centenary of his birth (Padua, 1508).

More recently, in 1951, the Italian Government donated the equestrian statues set nearby the Lincoln Memorial, and in 1962 another Roman architect, Luigi Walter Moretti designed the six buildings of the Watergate Complex.

The last, but not least, contribution has been the new building of the Italian Chancery, a modern Renaissance palace in the heart of the Capital's Embassy Row, already a landmark.

These and many others are the visible symbols of the friendship, presence and influence between the United States of America and Italy, and between our two people.

A friendship and solidarity that Alcide De Gasperi, the first Italian Prime Minister officially invited by the American Government to visit the United States, described as "essential between two Nations loving peace and freedom."

Let me express my personal gratitude to all the authors whose writings and research give this publication a relevant scientific and cultural depth.

I wish also to thank all the public and private institutions and companies whose generous support and contribution have enabled the realization of this prestigious publication.

Romano Prodi
Prime Minister of the Italian Republic

I am particularly pleased to present this praiseworthy publication devoted to the imprints which the Italian culture has left in the artistic and architectural landscape of the Capital of the United States.

The message at the center of the book, like the message emanating from the works of art whose beautiful pictures are featured in it, carries a powerful symbolic significance. It is the story, as the title of this publication aptly reminds us, of deep bonds and lasting friendship. In doing so, the book mirrors the very symbolism of a city, Washington, which exemplifies the ties of interdependence characterizing over two centuries of friendship between the two sides of the Atlantic.

This publication has also a more specific merit. It sheds some useful light on a chapter of the history of the Transatlantic relations which is less popular than others. A less known chapter but of no small significance: I am referring to the genius loci of the Capital of the newly independent American nation, for which Italy as a whole and Rome in particular offered a natural point of inspiration and reference.

The pages of this book provide a competent and captivating description of the influence Rome and Italy thus exerted on Washington, D.C., ranging from the shape of its buildings to the actual works which sculptors and painters coming from Italy contributed over the centuries. The story of the Italian imprints, in fact, extends well into our days: from the statues donated to the Lincoln Memorial in the 1950s to the architectural design of the Watergate Complex in the 1960s. The new building of the Italian Chancery in Washington is its latest and most appropriate example.

The readers will have ample opportunity to appreciate this book by themselves. I wish to express my personal appreciation to everyone, from the authors to the sponsors, who made this publication possible.

Massimo D'Alema
Deputy Prime Minister and Minister of Foreign Affairs of the Italian Republic

Buon giorno! As the first Mayor of the District of Columbia with Italian–American heritage, I'm delighted to introduce you to the important cultural contributions Italians have made to our Capital city.

Other American cities may have larger Italian populations than ours, but it's hard to visit a neighborhood in the District without seeing evidence of the artistic and architectural influences of Italy.

Beginning with the influence of Palladio, visitors to the District can see Italian-style architecture in some of our best-known buildings: the White House, the Capitol, the Washington Monument, Union Station and the Lincoln and Jefferson Memorials. Of course, no discussion of Italian architecture would be complete without mention of Moretti's Watergate Complex—now known as much for its impact on our political history as for its groundbreaking, curved facade.

Italy's roots run deep in the District of Columbia. This is a breathtaking book, and one I predict will become the very latest of the cultural jewels our nations have exchanged over time. Enjoy.

Sincerely,

Adrian M. Fenty
Mayor, Washington, D.C.

I was pleased when Ambassador Giovanni Castellaneta asked me to write an introduction on the presence of Italy in Washington, D.C. As someone who has lived in both places, I am continually struck by how deeply intertwined are the cultures of our two great countries.

The federal agency I head, the National Endowment for Humanities, is this nation's foremost supporter of studies of the Italian peninsula from its earliest civilizations to modern times. And the NEH, with the strong support of Ambassador Castellaneta, has recently concluded a memorandum of understanding with Italy's Consiglio Nazionale delle Ricerche to forge a strong transatlantic partnership.

This is fitting because the foundations of our two democracies rest on the heritage of ancient world and the Judeo–Christian tradition, a heritage rediscovered, preserved, and transmitted to us by the Italian Renaissance. Florence and Venice, along with other city-states, gave birth to many of our modern ideas about rationality, the worth of the individual, theories of governance, views of history, city planning, the importance of commerce and trade, exploration, and art and architecture.

From the city's inception in the early nineteenth century, Washington's architects have revered the buildings of the Renaissance and their ancient heritage as embodiments of stability, monumentality, order, and permanence—virtues associated with the Republic.

These ideas are given visual form all over Washington. Our great federal buildings and monuments—the Capitol, the White House, the National Gallery of Art (which contains one of the world's most distinguished collections of Italian painting), the National Archives, the Pension Building, the Supreme Court, and the agencies lining the Federal Triangle—derive their form and decoration from Italian prototypes.

This is true also for the monuments that adorn the city. Equestrian monuments in profusion grace the parks, circles, and squares of Washington. These statues, which depict some of the most consequential figures of American history, including George Washington, Nathaniel Greene, Andrew Jackson, Philip Sheridan, Ulysses S. Grant, and John Pershing, are the direct descendents of the Renaissance: their lines and proportions echo works by Donatello, Verrocchio, and Titian, who were in turn influenced by Roman prototypes. Many of American artists and architects, especially those of the nineteenth century, studied in Italy where they immersed themselves in the country's painting, sculpture, and architecture.

One of these students was the talented polymath Montgomery Meigs, whose service as Abraham Lincoln's masterful Quartermaster General helped the Union win the Civil War. Meigs' own home and his gigantic Pension Building are indebted to Renaissance domestic architecture. Meigs also commissioned Constantino Brumidi, an Italian immigrant, to decorate the interior of the Capitol with allegorical, historical, and decorative frescoes. With his paint brush, this new American transformed the heart of that storied building into a cathedral dedicated to democracy. Indeed, to see the profound influence of Italy in Washington one need only look to the U.S. Capitol with its great Pantheon-inspired rotunda and dome adorned by Brumidi's Apotheosis of George Washington.

America and Americans have had a long and fruitful friendship with Italy, so it's natural that Washington is the home to monuments celebrating great Italians. A monument to Columbus greets travelers at Union Station, a large bronze statue of Dante (a gift from Italy) broods in Meridian Hill Park, Leonardo da Vinci and Galileo grace the National Academy of Science building, and Guglielmo Marconi is honored on Sixteenth Street by one of Washington's most splendid Art Deco statues.

The influence of Italy—its design, fashion, cuisine, and architecture—continues to shape modern-day Washington. The famous Watergate Complex was designed by one of Italy's major twentieth-century architects. But it is the Chancery of Italy, whose exterior recalls a Renaissance palazzo and interior evokes sophisticated Italian modernism, which best represents present-day Italy in Washington.

At the entrance to Rock Creek Park are two large allegorical statues by James Earle Fraser representing "The Arts of Peace": Music and Harvest and Aspiration and Literature. Although the statues were begun before the Second World War, they were not completed until after that conflict ended. The statues were shipped to Italy to be cast and then given by the people of Italy to the people of the United States in 1951. In art and thought, these statues symbolize the important, enriching, and vital presence of Italy in Washington and throughout the United States. They also attest to the enduring cultural and intellectual ties shared by our two countries.

Bruce Cole
Chairman, National Endowment for the Humanities

When the tract along the Potomac that is now the District of Columbia was chosen as the site for the future capital of the United States, a grand plan was needed. The fathers of the American Constitution chose to give the city a strongly European flavor. You will read in the pages of this book how this idea translated into the conscious choice to adopt models from Italy. Indeed, the cultural influence of Italy was a determining factor in producing the final result, which incorporates many symbolic and cultural aspects proper to our country.

Classical architecture was chosen to provide the inspirational symbols of power in an attempt to graft the sobriety and values of Classical antiquity onto American puritan culture. Washington was to be the capital of the New World, a "new Rome" (aspiring to the Republican Rome of Cicero and Cato rather than to the Imperial Rome of Augustus and Nero) incarnating the lofty ideals of equality, liberty, democracy, harmony, and beauty.

Today, the Capital of the United States features a distinct profile and a clearly Classical style both architecturally and in its urban design. And the unmistakable Italian influence throughout its history from the eighteenth century to the present day is abundantly visible in every quarter of the city. You breathe it on Capitol Hill, the center of American legislative power, or among the Neoclassical villas in Kalorama. You find it in the names of many streets and neighborhoods in the city center and in the choice of construction materials, most notably the white Carrara marble.

In addition to being a source of artistic inspiration, Italy has also made a substantial contribution to creating the urban plan of Washington. The various migratory waves from Italy brought with them significant and varied contributions to the construction of the city. Italian immigrants were there when America was struggling for independence, and Italian workers, craftsmen, architects, engineers, sculptors, stonecutters, painters and artisans have been a constant presence ever since. They are among the major authors of the unique charm of this city on the banks of the Potomac, one that has been continuously enriched by Italian creativity and flair. From the mosaics in Saint Matthew's Cathedral to the curves of Luigi Moretti's Watergate Complex, the Italian touch is clearly recognizable.

While not boasting numbers similar to its counterparts in the large cities of the East Coast, the local Italian community has distinguished itself by its many contributions to the growth and development of the capital. Italy continues to leave a significant mark in America's capital in such areas as architecture, scientific research, universities, politics, and economics.

As Italian Ambassador to Washington, I often had the occasion—and the great fortune—to visit the marvels of the American Capital, to behold and enjoy its museums, theaters, and monuments. I recall with pleasure my recent visits to the Capitol, where I was filled with awe and pride before Pompeian paintings and the frescoes of Brumidi. I remember the Palladian-inspired villas scattered around the state of Virginia, designed by the brilliant hand of Thomas Jefferson, one of America's greatest lovers of Italian art, who benefited greatly from the guidance and suggestions of his friend, Filippo Mazzei. And I often took delightful strolls through the many Italian gardens in the Capital.

The great interest sparked by the Italian Chancery building in Washington provides further confirmation of the profound bond between the American capital and Italianate style. Its design was inspired by the Tuscan fortresses around Siena and symbolically represents the diamond shape of the city of Washington. It is thus a perfect symbol of the union between our two countries. Thanks to the innumerable cultural initiatives hosted there, the Chancery has become a new landmark for Washington art, culture, and politics.

This long and intense history of interaction and exchange begged the publication of a book examining the relationship between Italian artistry and the architecture of Washington, with a central focus on the new Italian Chancery. It has been made possible thanks to the invaluable contributions of experts from both the United States and Italy. I would especially like to thank, among my closest collaborators, First Counselor Luca Ferrari, Roberto Renna, and First Secretary Andrea Canepari, who supervised the project from beginning to end.

The bond of friendship between our country and the United States is rooted deep in the past and gains in strength and solidity with each passing day. With all its forms and hues, the architecture of Washington is one of the most salient symbols of the unity between our two countries. The dialogue between them, throughout the centuries of its history and on into the future, is based on a shared legacy of ideals and aspirations, and an identical sense of Republican sovereignty.

It is said that art is what remains when all the rest has been forgotten. The capital of the United States is deeply imbued with Italian art and artistry, and they will remain long into the future to represent the influence of Italian culture in the New World.

Giovanni Castellaneta
Ambassador of Italy in the United States

Contents

*Luca Molinari**

Italy–Washington: A Complex Tale

** Professor, Faculty of Architecture
"Luigi Vanvitelli", Naples*

Architecture is a powerful thing. It gives form to the physical and symbolic space that has marked humanity's progress from our origins to the present day. Architecture is a place where the knowledge and visions of different cultures meet, intermix, and enrich each other. It is a hybrid condition *par excellence*, where the architect's intuition and technical expertise interact first with the client, then with the builder, and lastly with the inhabitant.

In an era like our own, where everything seems to slip away inexorably, architecture has the power to stop time and to receive and accommodate the streams of life that pass through its spaces on a daily basis. A focus on the complex relationship between the two worlds of Italy and the United States, viewed through the lens of the architecture and art of Washington, D.C. as city and symbol, is perhaps the best way of interpreting the density and wealth of a cultural encounter involving knowledge exchange, stories, and large and small personalities that have gone into creating one of the most centrally important and recognizable urban centers in all of modern history.

This book represents the ambitious objective of giving recognizable form to some three centuries of American history as it has taken material form in large and small works that have shaped Washington's physical and intellectual landscape.

One will quickly grasp the meaning and richness of this encounter between two cultures just by leafing through the papers of Thomas Jefferson, the third President of the United States and one of the nation's preeminent founding fathers. In describing the interior of his Monticello, Jefferson wrote: "The Hall is in the Ionic, the Dining Room is in the Doric, the Parlor is in the Corinthian, and the Dome in the Attic. In the other rooms are introduced several different forms of those orders, all in the truest proportions according to Palladio." The culture and architectural style studied with care and devotion by Jefferson are those of Palladio and Italian Humanist Classicism. The books by the master from Vicenza were the centerpiece of Jefferson's library and influenced the nation's most important architectural and urban works; as we so clearly see in Washington, D.C., Italian Classicism and American pragmatism came together to give form and life to an autonomous and central current in the history of North American architectural culture, producing most of the governmental and public buildings in the city of Washington as in all of the major cities in the United States.

The essays by Livio Sacchi, Margherita Azzi Visentini, and Mario Valmarana provide a strong introduction to the theme of the rich and delicate relation between Palladian culture and the growth of an American Classicism out of a merger of local styles with a universal vision of architecture. From its beginnings in the eighteenth century, the American Classical style did not embrace solely the architecture of individual buildings but also represented a way of seeing and designing landscapes, gardens, and cities in a slow process of evolution that continues to this day.

An examination of Palladian stylistic and cultural influences overlies an interpreta-

Cherubino Gambardella, reinterpreting the Jefferson Memorial, 2007.

The National Archives, Washington,
detail of the facade.
Photo: Archivio Skira.

tion of the symbolic and rhetorical patrimony applied to the construction of the new capital of the United States of America. The essay by John E. Ziolkowski leads us through the dense web of relations existing between Washington, D.C. and the ideals of ancient republican Rome.

The history of Washington's architectural forms and symbols is not exclusively a tale of Classicism. Recent contributions have also marked the capital's contemporary architectural history. The Watergate Complex, in addition to having become a dramatic symbol in recent American political history, is also a milestone in the city's urban architectural history. Designed in the early 1960s by the Roman architect Luigi Moretti, it was the first large mixed public-private complex in which a decisively modern architectural style was introduced into a city that up to then had been exclusively characterized by the Classical Federal style. It might be thought of as a sort of beneficial cultural virus that brought a wind of change to this city and opened the way to the works of other contemporary American masters. The history of this building, introduced in Sacchi's essay, is also told through Luisa Vecchione's interview with Giuseppe Cecchi, who supervised the construction of the Watergate in the 1960s and is now one of the most active Italian builders in the capital.

A second, more recent work is the recently completed Chancery of the Italian Embassy, which was designed starting in 1992 by the Roman architect Piero Sartogo. It is another work of contemporary architecture that speaks with an Italian accent while carefully and respectfully interpreting the history and cityscape of Washington, D.C. This book allows us to become privy to the secrets of this important building thanks to conversations with its designer and with the man who built it, Leo Daly.

These two conversations are supplemented in an essay by Nathalie Grenon on the design collection created specially for the new Chancery, a true showcase of the best of contemporary Italian design. It provides an excellent representation of one of the contemporary currents where the bounty of Italian creativity is best manifested, as further attested by Paolo Scrivano's essay on the relationship between Italian design and contemporary American culture.

A second but equally important essay section is dedicated to the relationship between Italy and Washington that has developed within the sphere of art. In order to begin naming the constellations in this vast universe, we invited Barbara Wolanin to introduce us to the works of Constantino Brumidi and other worthy Italian artists and artisans who contributed to building and embellishing the Capitol. David Alan Brown and Maygene Daniels provide discerning insights into the contents and development of the Italian art collection at the Washington National Museum of Modern Art.

We close the volume with an essay by Ennio Caretto, who looks at the long history of exchange and interrelation between Italy and America from the viewpoint of the many Italians, famous or not, who contributed their life, work, and experience to the construction of Washington, D.C.

The book is embellished throughout with photographs created specially by Max McKenzie, telling the tale of other places and less famous (but no less important) events in the relationship between Italy and Washington. He takes us on a tour of Jefferson's architectural works from Barboursville to Monticello and then on to the Watergate Complex and the new Italian Chancery. He shows us Brumidi's spectacular frescoes in the U.S. Capitol, the Italian church in Washington, the bronze equestrian sculptures donated to Washington by the Republic of Italy in 1953, and closes with Villa Florence, residence of the Italian Ambassador to the United States and a place where Italian, European, and American culture come together in a unique and exemplary natural setting.

*Livio Sacchi**

Jefferson & Co.
The Influence of the Italian Architectural Culture in Washington, D.C. and Virginia

* *Professor of Architectural Design, Faculty of Architecture, University of Pescara–Chieti*

The cultural inclinations of the United States of America before, during and after the Revolution of 1776 can generally be summed up as an attempt to graft Classical antiquity onto New-World Puritan piety. Paradoxically, the new *Homo americanus* needed well-defined roots in some near or remote past. And true to the Renaissance spirit, the immediate impulse was to look to antiquity, especially to Rome. It was not a question of indiscriminately copying all things Roman, but rather an attempt to capture the essence and transport the principles of the virtuous Republican age (not those of the decadent Imperial age) into the present. Puritanism and neo-Classicism did share a clear radicalism and a strong innovative thrust that came together to produce a stylistic attitude that was permeated—in art and particularly in architecture—by a didactic, moralizing stoicism, by ethical thought centered on the infallibility of divinely illuminated reason. But what did Americans know, in the middle of the eighteenth century, about Classical antiquity? What had reached them of all the intervening history of Europe? Not much actually, even though the paucity of what did get there was amply compensated by the keen desire and diligence, characteristic of people who feel they are far from the center, to recover something that seems to have been lost from their cultural baggage. Take for example the case of Benjamin West, a promising American painter who could find no teachers or schools and so decided, at the tender age of twenty-two, to board the good ship *Betty Sally* and sail—where else?—to Rome. There he found a more recent and extraordinary artistic tradition, developing over the previous three centuries, that had reworked and superseded that of Classical antiquity. Here Cardinal Alessandro Albani, the blind arbiter of the Roman art scene, expecting to find himself in the presence of a savage, touched the face of the youth and recognized "the head of a true painter." Taken to the Vatican where he beheld the *Apollo Belvedere*, West exclaimed: "How like a young Mohawk warrior!," perhaps unwittingly echoing a curious opinion expressed some years prior by Winckelmann.[1]

The architectural protagonist of our story is Thomas Jefferson (1743–1826), third President of the United States, in office from 1801 to 1809. His quest, which we may generally summarize as political, religious, and intellectual freedom, was based on the exaltation of a natural aristocracy—not, as in corrupt Europe, on the privileges of birth or wealth, but exclusively on merit. This apostle of equality was well aware that slavery was an "abominable crime," although this did not stop him, in 1796, from finding himself the owner of some 170 slaves. On the educational role of the arts Jefferson harbored no doubts, although he did have doubts about their practical value in the American context. He wrote in 1788 to some friends who were traveling to Europe that painting and sculpture were "too expensive for the state of wealth among us" and worth seeing but not studying. He was not alone in this viewpoint. Benjamin Franklin did not see a need to import art from Italy, he hoped rather that Americans could obtain the recipe for making Parmesan cheese.[2] But none of this held true for architecture. Jefferson—lawyer, farmer, revolutionary, diplomat, and statesman—spent a great deal of time studying architecture. "Architecture shows so

much," he wrote, and so do all of his buildings.[3] His cultural foundations in general and his architectural background in particular are permeated by Classicism, a classicism deriving first and foremost from his studies (at the age of twenty-two he had already bought Palladio's treatise in a 1721 edition published by Giacomo Leoni, and he took pleasure in translating from Greek and Latin the descriptions of Plinius's Roman villa and Hadrian's villa at Tivoli). But it was also instilled by the books in the library assembled by William Byrd in Westover (twenty-six volumes dedicated to architecture, including Palladio's *Four Books on Architecture*), by King-George-style Williamsburg (which he did not like, but he studied at the College of William and Mary, where legend has it that the main building had been designed by none other than Christopher Wren) and by his European travels during his five years (1784–89) as American Minister to France, a post he inherited from Benjamin Franklin, shortly after the end of the American Revolution and shortly before the beginning of its French counterpart. He was the greatest architect of his generation and his tastes in architecture—anglophobe that he was—naturally repudiated the

English models. He found the buildings of London to be inferior to those of Philadelphia. His love was for Paris and France in general. The building he loved more than any other was in France, but it was not a French building. It was the Maison Carrée, a Roman temple from the Augustan age, greatly admired by Nicolas Poussin, among others. Jefferson's European peregrinations took him as far as Genoa (apparently to observe rice cultivation), but he never reached Rome. His knowledge of Roman architecture was thus book-learned or otherwise derivative. Progressively distancing himself from English culture, and from what English culture had gleaned from Classicism and exported to America, Jefferson moved closer to the ideals of republican France and pre-imperial Rome. Although he lacked formal academic training in the field, he was an architect in the fullest sense of the word. He designed buildings (Monticello), groups of buildings (the University of Virginia campus), pieces of cities (Washington), and entire urban plans (Richmond, Virginia). For the new federal capital he actively promoted and supported the urban design work of L'Enfant and the architectural work of Benjamin Henry Latrobe, who was then superintendent of public buildings. Palladio's influence on Jefferson was enormous and has remained so for American architectural culture in general. Jefferson ended up owning five editions of Palladio's famous architectural treatise, which he referred to as "my Bible." Monticello, the Capitol in Richmond, and the University of Virginia, his three masterpieces, may all be to some extent attributed to Palladio's influence.

Monticello was his first work. Taking a clear distance from historical precedents on American soil, Jefferson built his house on a 850-foot-high hilltop overlooking the Rivanna River valley not far from Charlottesville in a stunning natural setting at the heart of a broad plantation inherited from his father. And since Palladio wrote that Villa Rotonda was positioned "*sopra un monticello*" [atop a small mountain], Jefferson named his house "Monticello." The first phase of construction took place in 1769–75 in clearly Palladian style yet with perceptible Georgian influences. Monticello was completed in 1782 (the year his wife, Martha, died) but underwent radical modifications until 1808 according to the dictates of the Roman Revival style, however with French nuances. Jefferson never ceased modifying his creation until his death on July 4, 1826. It was, as we said, a masterpiece, a Palladian dream transferred to Virginia. Looking at the floor plan, the living and dining areas are clearly distinguished from the service areas, setting a precedent for a separation that would become dear to Louis Kahn. The latter are designed as detached, linear wings that are almost invisible to visitors (all one sees are the rooftop terraces). They connect to the main house via sunken "all-weather" passageways. The main house has a much more complex cruciform floor plan that does not lack in ambiguity. It is difficult to grasp its form without walking around it carefully. The two floors do not always appear to be adequately resolved on the facade. The low central dome over Jefferson's favorite room, his octagonal *Sky Room*, is visible only from the upper floor when you are inside the house. Externally, the contrast between the white of the Classical trim and the red of the brick walls is a bit ingenuous in its application of a typical Georgian stylistic element, but the portico and the dome function as catalysts and the resulting image is altogether impressive and uplifting. The interiors are particularly charming. The fixtures exhibit a detailed array of Roman styles. The Classical friezes, no two of which are alike, are all taken from important publications, mainly English and French, and inspired to some extent by Palladio. Jefferson wrote: "The Hall is in the Ionic, the Dining Room is in the Doric, the Parlor is in the Corinthian, and the Dome in the Attic. In the other rooms are introduced several different forms of those orders, all in the truest proportions according to Palladio."[4] Monticello also heralds a typically American peculiarity, that of blending with nonchalance a love of Classicism with a desire for modern comforts. The house was full of clever devices and mechanisms ranging from the automatic doors to the forced-air ventilation ducts, and even contained a machine for copying letters, a sort of Xerox machine *ante litteram*.

The Virginia State Capitol in Richmond was completed in 1792. Jefferson had had his hand in this project since 1785, and dictated the rules of the game once and for all, firmly establishing the prototype for American Roman Revival style, the federal style, one which could neither be colonial nor seem beholden to tyranny, but rather had to evoke republican virtues. The reference to Maison Carrée is clear, in spite of the fact that the proportions are different, the facade wider and the simpler Ionic order is preferred (in non-tapering columns) to the Corinthian of the Roman original. Actually, the famous temple, which Jefferson visited personally and with much devotion in Nîmes, was a product of Cae-

Thomas Jefferson, University of Virginia, 1817–26, wooden model of the Rotunda. Photo: Livio Sacchi.

The U.S. Capitol viewed from the Mall.
Photo: Archivio Skira.

sarean Rome and not of the Republic. Furthermore, given the fact that it stands on French soil, it must be considered a colonial building. By conceiving a similar building in Richmond, Jefferson hoped to demonstrate a grandeur of conception, "republican simplicity" and "true elegance of proportion" proper to a tempered liberty that admits no frivolity or food for small minds.[5] It was thus the first public building complex in the history of American architecture purposely adhering to the form of a Classic temple. For a long time afterwards the Classical language of architecture was the only conceivable option for this type of building. With all its defects, even if merely in terms of execution, the Capitol was so highly paradigmatic that it would be destined to play a seminal role in all of subsequent American architecture (starting with the Capitol building in Washington, D.C., where work would begin the following year). The building we see today differs in a number of respects from the original: the two wings for the Senate and the House of Representatives were added in the early 1900s (1904–06), and the south portico has been modified. Additional modifications, both exterior and interior, were made in the early 1960s. What remains is unquestionably the refinement of its stylistic choices, the discernment of its setting and the elegance of the grounds.

The University of Virginia at Charlottesville (1817–26), America's first non-religious university, was Jefferson's last work. It was completed a year after his death (and later broadly reworked). The cornerstone was laid on October 6, 1817 in the presence of three presidents: Jefferson, Madison, and Monroe. It is a grand campus, a true classical village of culture immersed in greenery, laid out in a stately rectangle enclosing the broad Lawn, a huge green plaza encircled by rows of trees and ten colonnaded dormitories for students and instructors. The buildings were conceived as a sort of museum of Classical orders: the Doric of the Baths of Diocletian, the Ionic of the Temple of Virile Fortune, etc. A

second outer row of buildings, the Range, housing graduate students, alternates with botanical gardens and outdoor teaching areas. The campus is dominated by the elegant Rotunda, the symbolic center of the entire complex, crowned with a low dome and characterized by a facade with two hexastyle porticoes: one facing the Lawn, the other facing off-campus. It is a temple of culture, the materialization of an ancient humanistic dream transplanted into the heart of America. Jefferson was convinced that the American university system had to be based on a secular model, as opposed to the religious foundations of the earliest Puritan institutions in Massachusetts, which had been established along the lines of Oxford and Cambridge. The architecture—for which Jefferson sought guidance in Benjamin Latrobe, who would be one of the future architects of the Capitol building in Washington—is coherent with the new educational order. Unlike Harvard, Princeton, King's College (the original name of Columbia), or the College of William and Mary, all founded on the primacy of theology in higher education, Charlottesville was a truly humanistic university strongly grounded in the concepts of beauty, liberty, justice, and equality. The Rotunda, standing on a tiered stylobate, was clearly inspired by the Pantheon. Half as big, it maintains the same proportions. A sphere can be perfectly inscribed in its interior. Considered by its author to be "the most perfect" of the campus buildings, work was begun on it in 1823 and completed two years later. It was devastated by a fire in 1895 and later rebuilt, somewhat modified, by Stanford White. Working with the McKim, Mead & White studio, he also designed the building erected in 1896–98 that, perhaps unfortunately, closes off the rectangle of the Lawn, which had originally given onto a stunningly beautiful landscape.

The Founding Fathers could have chosen any large American city, such as New York or Philadelphia, for the new federal capital. But that would have meant an unfair advantage for one State and inevitably have had colonial or royalist undertones. Thus they opted for a newly founded city and, in 1791, the choice fell to a climatically inhospitable place, a hot and humid tract along the Potomac River. That same year, Jefferson entrusted the design to a French military engineer and son of a painter who had worked in Versailles for the king: Pierre Charles L'Enfant. Arriving in America in 1777, L'Enfant had been a volunteer in the wars of the young democracy. He placed the two most important buildings, the Capitol and the presidential residence, on two hills in an otherwise flat area, one to the north and the other to the east of a small stream with the Roman and somewhat rhetorical name "Tiber Creek." The influence of Classicism à la Palladio was enormous in the new city, leaving an indelible mark that remains to this day its main characterizing element. Examples include the White House (built in its original version in 1792, but later rebuilt in 1815); the United States Capitol (1793–1863); the Washington Monument, the gigantic obelisk by Robert Mills (1848–85); the curious National Building Museum (formerly the Pension Building) by Montgomery C. Meigs (1882–87), a rhapsody of arches and superimposed orders that clearly and somewhat superficially repropose the drawings by Sangallo and Michelangelo for the Palazzo Farnese in Rome; Union Station by Daniel H. Burnham (1903–08), an elegant Beaux-Arts work designed by the architect ten years after the famous World's Columbian Exhibition in Chicago; and the Lincoln Memorial by Henry Bacon (1915–22), a temple in white marble marked by a Roman *gravitas* that is softened by its airy and green setting. Henry-Russell Hitchcock saw a sort of perennial neo-Classicism in the Lincoln Memorial, as rigorous as that of 1880.[6] Hitchcock had had long experience with that style and was relieved that not all of the traditional architecture built in the years from 1900 to 1930 had to be dismissed scornfully, even though the criteria by which it must be judged continue to be those of the nineteenth rather than the twentieth century.[7] In the late nineteenth and the first decades of the twentieth century, the best examples of Classicism—i.e., those that were most carefully designed, better built, and generally more concerned about providing an interpretation of "good taste"—were thus built on American rather than European soil (with the possible exception of the works of Sir Edwin Lutyens in England). Paradoxically, no Italian architect would have been able to provide as cultured and balanced an architectural interpretation of the sixteenth century in Italy as the American Academy, built in 1913 on the Gianicolo Hill in Rome by McKim, Mead & White. But it may also be true that no Italian architect of the time would have been interested in undertaking such a challenge.

We could go on to later architecture, that built in the years of the Second World War, represented by bona fide—and in certain ways quite embarrassing—cases of stylistic survival, such as the nevertheless magnificent National Gallery of Art (1941) and the Jefferson Memorial (1943), both the work of John Russell Pope. The latter is another Pantheon, this time brilliantly white. Reflected in the calm waters of the Potomac Tidal Basin, it offers some of the most beautiful tourist photos that can be shot in Washington, D.C. today. Pope was the true champion of American National Classicism, which in those years shared the stage with the Modern Movement, then at its apex, at least in terms of theoretical propositions. In 1895, one year after receiving his degree from Columbia, Pope won the first scholarship from the American School of Architecture in Rome. He stayed there eighteen months, during which he discovered and studied the Theater of Marcellus, under the guidance of Charles McKim. McKim helped consolidate the conviction in the budding architect that design had to be grounded in Classicism and, in particular, in a Classicism based on the Italian Renaissance and its illustrious precedents in republican and imperial Rome. It was not a simple question of taste, but a clear-sighted effort to provide legitimacy for contemporary works while maintaining substantial continuity with the very origins of Western civilization. Pope's work initially met with significant applause even among such die-hard modernists as Lewis Mumford. It comes as no surprise that he was called to London to work on the British Museum and the Tate Gallery.[8]

He presented two rather similar proposals for the Jefferson Memorial. One was based, yet again, on the Pantheon, while the other was a further evocation of Palladio's Rotonda. The architect justified his choices on the basis of Jefferson's interest in both buildings. He accompanied his plans with a photograph of the Rotunda at the University of Virginia. The final project was approved by President Roosevelt in 1937. But the country had encountered difficult economic times, and the plan began to suffer heavy attack, first of all from the ranks of the Modernists, from William Lescaze to Mumford himself. Frank Lloyd Wright, in a letter to Roosevelt, called the Memorial an "arrogant insult to the memory of Thomas Jefferson," whom he praised as a cultured democrat, loved by many and respected by all. Wright saw Mr. Pope as the latest Washington fashion and bewailed the way his works forced one to fake positive feelings for the present when one was actually standing before a morgue.[9] Funds were frozen and it was not until after Pope's death in 1937 that the executive designs were finally completed by his colleagues. Plans for the National Gallery were drawn up in at least two dozen different versions which were later reduced to six. The final version substantially echoed McKim, Mead & White's Brooklyn Museum, as well as a number of French projects prepared for the Prix de Rome. Here again, the building was completed after the death of its designer and not without heated debate between the supporters and detractors of Classicism. Pope won, but it was really too late.

Italian influence in Washington did not end with the final eclipse of Classicism. In the second half of the twentieth century at least two other noted Italian architects met with success in the city. We are referring to Luigi Moretti, architect of the Watergate Complex, built in the 1960s, and to Piero Sartogo, who designed the Chancery of the Italian Embassy. The Watergate (1961–63), designed by Moretti along with the studio of Corning, Elmore, Fisher & Moore, was built exactly ten years after his building on Corso Italia in

Watergate Complex, detail of the
Potomac side.

Milan, one of Moretti's masterpieces. These were the international years for the Italian architect. In the same period he designed the Stock Exchange Tower in Montreal and immediately afterward was asked to design buildings in the Holy Land, in Kuwait, and in Algeria. In 1971, he was asked to design the Madrid exhibition. The Watergate Complex, made famous by the scandal that toppled the Richard Nixon presidency, is characterized by its curvilinear design. While not matching their elegance, it has a number of important precedents: the eighteenth-century Royal Crescent in Bath, Le Corbusier's projects for the large residential units planned for Algiers, and perhaps even the New York Guggenheim. These were not kind years for facades. Just think of the coeval works of American architects such as Minoru Yamasaki or Edward Durrell Stone. But in the Watergate they are treated like a single, colossal molding, expanding the plasticity of Baroque lines onto the urban scale with expressionist effects. Nevertheless, our positive judgment of the Watergate Complex is not limited to its curves. We also admire the power of its space-enclosing volumes and their capacity to highlight a large public space on the urban scale. Even more, we are impressed by its relationship with the landscape, which slopes gently down to the river.

Lastly, the Chancery of the Italian Embassy is one of a long line of diplomatic buildings, generally concentrated along Embassy Row, near Massachusetts Avenue, designed by famous architects: Sir Edwin Lutyens (Embassy of the United Kingdom, 1925–28), Egon Eiermann and Oswald Mathias Ungers (German Embassy, 1964, and Ambassador's residence, 1994), Heikkinen-Komonen (Finnish Embassy, 1994), Steven Holl (Swiss Embassy, 2004), to name just a few. The winning plan in a design contest, the building designed by Sartogo is based on a regular layout cut in half by an asymmetrical diagonal. The cut opens a forced perspective that attenuates the external impact of the massive volume and exalts the richness and complexity of its interior space. The interior is characterized by a spacious, glass-roofed two-story atrium that functions not only as an entrance and distributive node for the different parts of the building, but also as a meeting and exhibition space. The facades are faced in brick. The broad overhang of the roof creates a strong shadow marking the edge where the building meets the sky.

[1] R. Hughes, *American Visions, The Epic History of Art in America* (New York: Alfred A. Knopf, 1997), pp. 71–72.
[2] Ibid., p. 109.
[3] Ibid., p. 110.
[4] G. E. Kidder Smith, *Source Book of American Architecture*, Princeton Architectural Press, New York 1996, p. 111.
[5] Hughes, *American Visions*, p. 112.
[6] Henry-Russell Hitchcock, *Architecture: Nineteenth and Twentieth Centuries* (Harmondsworth: Penguin, 1958).
[7] Ibid., p. 535.
[8] L. Mumford, *Sticks and Stones* (New York, 1924), p. 148.
[9] Letter from Frank Lloyd Wright to Franklin Delano Roosevelt, Taliesin Spring Green, March 30, 1937, kept in the "F. D. Roosevelt Papers", New York, Franklin D. Roosevelt Presidential Library, Hyde Park.

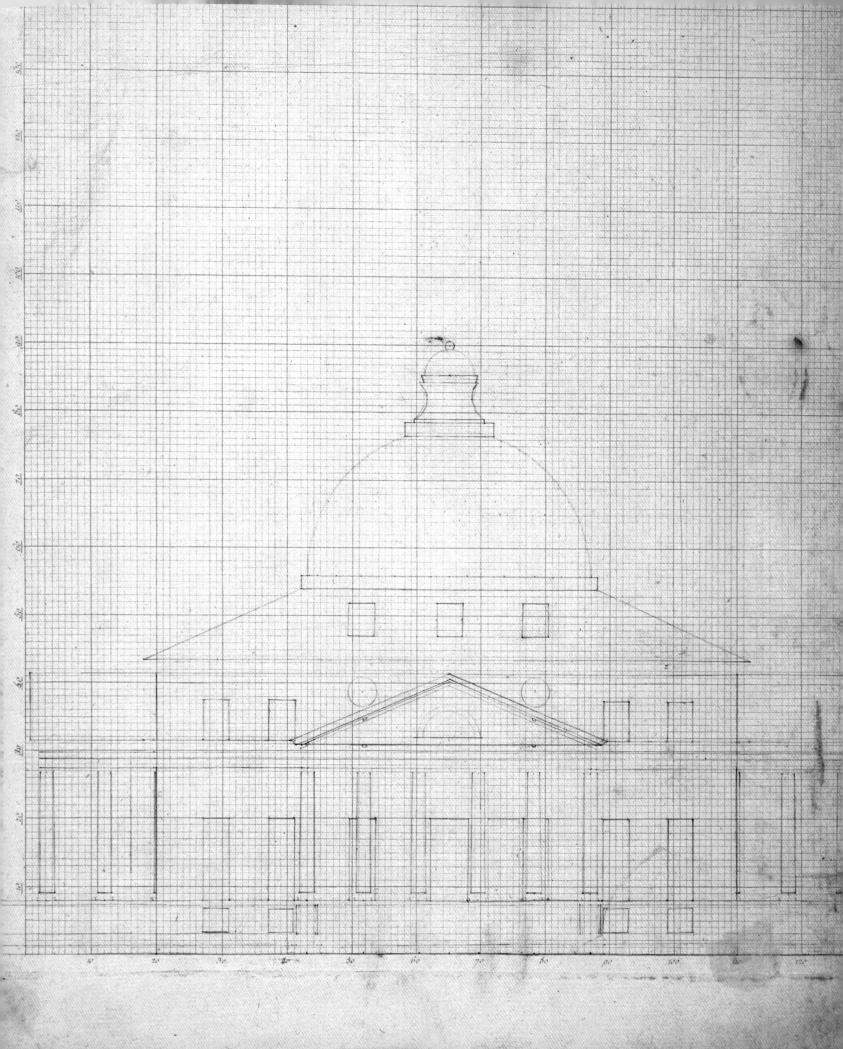

Mario Valmarana*

Palladianism in the United States of America

* Professor, Faculty of Architecture,
University of Virginia

Foreword

A coherent evaluation of "Palladianism in America" within the critical and historical framework of the development of American culture must consider three distinct periods. The first period was characterized by British cultural dominance in the early colonies from the mid-seventeenth century up to the Revolution of 1776, and thus took form along the eastern seaboard of the newly forming nation. This period was marked by intense development of colonial architecture and substantially set a lasting standard for homes in New England. At the time, knowledge of Palladian architecture in the New World was rooted in the theoretical repertory formulated by Inigo Jones in England, and in the formal and academic interpretation of a large and rather self-absorbed body of architectural literature that was inaccessible to American popular culture and thus not something that could be transmitted to the various social classes.

The second period extends from the explosive events that led to the formation of the Republic to the dawn of the American Renaissance in 1880. It was ushered in when Thomas Jefferson introduced and developed the Palladian scheme as a rebuttal to British culture, mainly based on the teachings he had drawn from the great literary opus, *Four Books on Architecture*, of the master from Vicenza. Jefferson embraced the humanistic notion of the Italian Renaissance, and introduced Palladianism onto the North American continent as the true national style, something that could be assimilated by all social strata. At the time, the competing French style, which carried strong political overtones in those times, was relegated to the margins, suitable only for very stately applications. It would gain vigor only later when the Ecole des Beaux-Arts emerged on the scene and American architectural culture began to acquire international characteristics.

The third period stretches up to the present, and is perhaps the most complex and delicate period in American architecture. Palladio's style emerges and disappears depending on the styles of the moment, and it is very difficult to assign it a precise role. From the advent of the International Renaissance in 1880, the neo-Classical revivals (erroneously termed Palladian) of the first quarter of the twentieth century, the New York debut of International Style mediated by Johnson and Hitchcock, and the misfortunes of the modern era up to the current "postmodern" age, the developmental events in architecture find little resonance with Palladian culture.

In writing this chapter on Palladianism in America, I have sought to present architectural examples that are best suited to conveying, although necessarily in a somewhat limited way, the evolution of Palladio's style in the United States, choosing what may be considered the crowning examples in an inexhaustible series of Palladian structures. I have cited works that will appeal to the curious reader without going into all the complex analytical and historical detail that would be demanded by a more exhaustive discussion of Palladio's influence in the United States.

Thomas Jefferson, study for elevation
of the President's House, Washington, 1792.

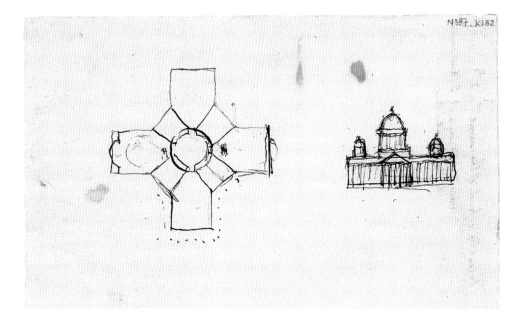

Palladio's Influence in American Architecture

Palladio has always been considered the most influential architect of all time. The Europeans admired his works, especially in England, where his designs, acquired by Inigo Jones 32 years after the death of the master from Vicenza, were eagerly reviewed and analyzed, and his *Four Books on Architecture*, translated into various languages, were thoroughly studied. The enthusiastic Lord Burlington, nicknamed the "architecture earl" was instrumental in the revival of Palladian architecture, offering a rigorous interpretation of its essential principles.

With their colonial expansion in the sixteenth century, the European countries exported Palladian taste to the various continents and made it a universally recognized style. His works first reached the North American colonies with the translation of Palladio's *Quattro Libri* [Four Books] and in such literary-architectural works as Colen Campbell's *Vitruvius Britannicus* (1727) and the *Book of Architecture* (1728) by James Gibbs, which presented a new interpretation of the Palladian concept. It should be pointed out that Palladio's contemporary architect colleagues were often completely oblivious of the true spirit underlying his message.

At this point it would be opportune to illustrate briefly the development of architecture in the United States. The seventeenth was the Jacobean century, characterized by Medieval architecture with Renaissance embellishments introduced from England and establishing a "new style." This would give rise to the King George (or Georgian) style that dominated the eastern seaboard for three quarters of a century.

The first forty years of the next century was the period of the Early Georgian style, exemplified by Drayton Hall. This was followed by the High Georgian, which represented a Palladian style as had been absorbed by and filtered through Burlington, Campbell, and Gibbs. This would become the fashionable style, as demonstrated by Mount Airy. Finally there was the Late Georgian period in architecture, which would continue after the 1776 Revolution. It is characterized by compartmentalized structure, as we see in the Hammond-Harwood House. This was followed in turn by the Federal style, also known as the Adamesque, Pompeian, or neo-Classical style. Jefferson emerged in this period with his Roman Classical style, exemplified in the University of Virginia. It would spark a chain reaction throughout the U.S. territory, especially in the South, where the Classical portico, while becoming an aesthetic symbol, also served a very functional purpose in the sultry local climate. The Greek war of independence of 1820 stimulated a flourishing Greek Revival, which had broad echoes in the southern States.

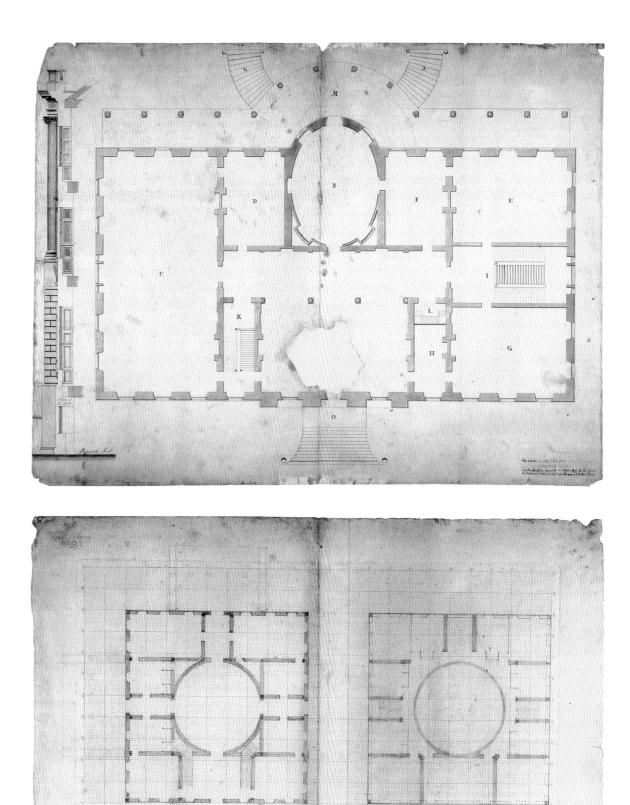

Thomas Jefferson, President's House study plans, Washington, 1792.

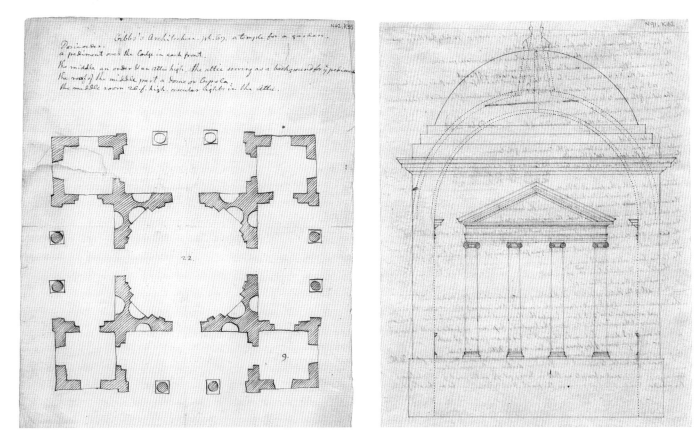

Thomas Jefferson, Garden Temple, 1779–81; Ionic Portico and Dome, Monticello, 1778.

Thomas Jefferson, Observation Tower, Monticello, 1771.

Starting in 1840, a new freer and more informal trend in architectural expression began to supplant that adhering to the rigid dogmatic criteria of symmetry that had become *de rigueur* in American architecture. The Palladian concept of the correspondence between external expression and internal function, of the intimate relation between landscape and architecture, became a fundamental element—as demonstrated by Lyndhurst in Tarrytown, New York and Llewellyn Park, New Jersey—and would later be formalized by two eminent architects out of the Ecole des Beaux-Arts of Paris, H. H. Richardson and R. M. Hunt.

In the meantime, the Italianate villa and Second Empire (Napoleon III) styles had become favorites in America.

In 1893, the Chicago World's Fair launched Classical Revival in the arts, while the architects McKim, Mead & White rediscovered the neo-Colonial style in New England, a style which would last until the First World War. In 1932, International Style was introduced in New York by Philip Johnson and Henry Hitchcock, a style which had already been formulated in Europe prior to the war.

Beyond the consequences for formal values that this episode would bring to American architectural culture, it initiated a literary reaction that would be of paramount importance for Palladianism in the United States. Rudolph Wittkower's *Architectural Principles in the Age of Humanism*, published in 1949, illustrates the Palladian system of proportions as a response to the concept of "form follows function." We are thus at the threshold of a new Palladian revival.

Early Palladianism

British Palladianism was introduced to America by Peter Harrison in 1749 in the Redwood Library. Its temple-like design derived literally from Edward Hoppus's 1773 book *Palladio*, and from *Design from Inigo Jones and Others* (1740) by Isaac Ware. Harrison was born in England and influenced by Lord Burlington. We may observe his Palladian tendency in the

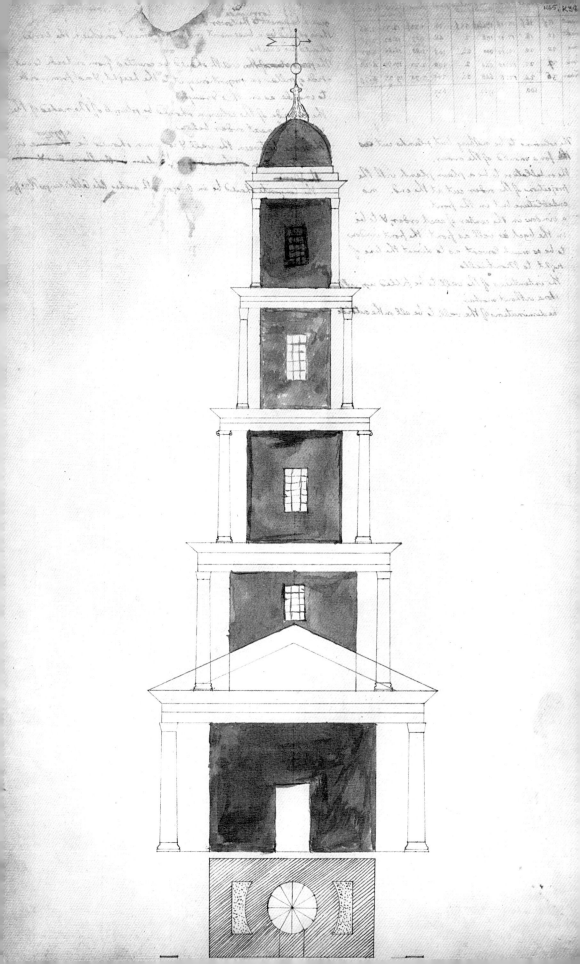

Brick Market (1761–62) in Newport, Rhode Island. Here we note the overlarge proportions of the architectural order, based on Inigo Jones's Old Somerset House in London.

The first private building with a portico (thus with the form of a temple) was Whitehall in Maryland, although it was too stately to catch on as a model for others. It was only later, with Jefferson's designs for the Capitol in Richmond, Virginia, that the portico as an integral part of a private dwelling began gaining in popularity. Another Palladian type of this period was the plantation house composed of three or five units. Initially the outlying units were not connected to the central building in order to reduce the risk of fire (the kitchen facilities were distanced from the main building for this and other reasons). It was only later that unitary structures with clear Palladian flavor were built, as we see in the innumerable examples from the late eighteenth century.

Jefferson and Romantic Classicism

During his diplomatic mission to France (1784–89), Thomas Jefferson (1743–1826) not only encountered examples of Roman antiquity (in Nîmes), but also the contemporary French buildings of two eminent architects, L. E. Boullée and C. N. Ledoux, who were the fathers of French romantic Classicism (as opposed to English picturesque Classicism), which provided Jefferson with his inspiration for his later architectural production.

Jefferson's main goal was to Romanize the United States by means of Roman Classicism. His source for cultural innovation was Palladio, whom Jefferson revered as his master. He referred to Palladio's *Four Books on Architecture* (of which he possessed five copies) as his "Bible." Charged with a new ideal of liberty and mindful of the need to develop a culture that diverged from its British forebear, Jefferson set to work, offering the new nation an architecture inspired by Classic canons (the University of Virginia) that could be successfully reproduced at all levels of society. He sought to orient new generations towards a humanistic spirit, independent of any organized system, whether ecclesiastic or industrial. Not only do Jefferson's literary works provide examples of his unflagging efforts to affirm these principles, but also his architecture. He referred to the University of Virginia—with its Rotunda, the Pavilions, the student dormitories and the Lawn—as an "academic village," standing in opposition to the industrial villages that were rapidly spreading across the landscape in those times. Jefferson's intention was to prepare the future generations intellectually and culturally to resist any form of bondage, inspired by the Classic and humanistic spirit embodied in the pursuit of happiness. The forms of the many university buildings show a clear Palladian heritage, as may be noted especially in Pavilions III, V, and VII.

In order to achieve this humanistic ideal, it was necessary to work in an agrarian democracy, for which Monticello was to be the symbol. The agrarian village, parallel to the academic village, was to be productive, independent of the industrial system, self-sufficient, and economically viable. The organizational system of the agricultural village, which could be extended to the entire United States, was to be a

Thomas Jefferson, study for elevation, Barboursville, 1817.

challenge to the industrial system. But it was a challenge that was fated to remain a utopia, although it did stimulate a number of other utopian responses of great literary merit. It is thus obvious that almost all of Jefferson's architectural production focuses on the country house rather than on its urban counterpart. Barboursville, Poplar Forest, and Edgemont are all examples of this. His architecture exceeds the most daring expectations. The barriers of regionalism are completely removed to give rise to a dialogue of styles and forms. We find Maryland's High Georgian style on Long Island, New York, Virginia's style in Texas, New England style invading the southern States, and models of Mount Vernon and Monticello all over the United States. The national style has become a reality.

Colonial Revival and Late Palladianism

During the "battle of the styles" that erupted in the years following the Civil War (1861–65), the spread of Palladio's style came to a momentary halt, lasting until the emergence of the Colonial Revival style in the late nineteenth century. This revival was an invention of the architecture studio of McKim, Mead & White, who "rediscovered" the classical elements and used them as a model for a new architecture that would have a broad echo across the United States.

The new Classic Revival was followed by another inspired by the Ecole des Beaux-Arts, which embodied a more complex culture and more sophisticated quality than Colonial Revival. This elegant and refined Palladianism (if we may still call it by this name) of exquisitely French taste was quite popular up to the Second World War. The architecture between the two wars was characterized by a Georgian revival of academic taste, and examples abound. The country house predominates as a getaway and not a place for agricultural production, as Jefferson would have preferred. Eminent architects such as Charles Platt, William Delano, John Aldrich, William Bottomley, and John R. Pope with their impeccable formal works demonstrate an academic eclecticism lacking in a clear Palladian theme.

After the Second World War, Palladianism was represented in literary works. In 1947 the historian Colin Rowe, in *The Mathematics of the Ideal Villa*, made important comparisons between Le Corbusier (Villa Savoye) and Palladio (Villa Malcontenta), and incited a new Palladian awareness based on the natural beauty of mathematical principles. As stated above, Palladianism reached the threshold of a new revival. Perhaps it will be what we refer to today as "postmodern."

Thomas Jefferson
Monticello Estate
Charlottesville

1769–1808

The front portico to the manor.
The servants' quarters and stalls
can be seen in the background.

The manor viewed from the gardens.

Detail of the principal axis uniting the main rooms of the manor.

Monticello was Jefferson's first work. Taking a clear distance from historical precedents on American soil, Jefferson built his house on a 850-foot-high hilltop overlooking the Rivanna River valley not far from Charlottesville in a stunning natural setting at the heart of a broad plantation inherited from his father.

And since Palladio wrote that Villa Rotonda was positioned "*sopra un monticello*" [atop a small mountain], Jefferson named his house "Monticello." The first phase of construction took place in 1769–75 in clearly Palladian style yet with perceptible Georgian influences. Monticello was completed in 1782 (the year Jefferson's wife, Martha, died) but underwent radical modifications until 1808 according to the dictates of the Roman Revival style, however with French nuances. Jefferson never ceased modifying his creation until his death on July 4, 1826. It is a recognized masterpiece, a Palladian dream transferred to Virginia. Looking at the floor plan, the living and dining areas are clearly distinguished from the service areas. The latter are designed as detached, linear wings that are almost invisible to visitors (all one sees are the rooftop terraces). They connect to the main house via sunken "all-weather" passageways. The main house has a much more complex cruciform floor plan with a large portico and a shallow dome crowning the central octagonal hall. The interiors are particularly charming. The fixtures exhibit a detailed array of Roman styles. The Classical friezes, no two of which are alike, are all taken from important publications, mainly English and French, and inspired to some extent by Palladio. Monticello also heralds a typically American peculiarity, that of blending with nonchalance a love of Classicism with a desire for modern comforts. The house was full of clever devices and mechanisms ranging from the automatic doors to the forced-air ventilation ducts, and even contained a machine for copying letters, a sort of Xerox machine *ante litteram*.

Detail of the alcove, nestled between
the main rooms of the manor.

Thomas Jefferson
Governor Barbour
Residence
Barboursville
1814

Aerial view of the ruined villa
and the restored residences.
© Zonin Estate.

The two main facades. The columns stood at the entrance to the main, two-story octagonal hall.

The ruins that can be visited today are what remains of an imposing villa designed by Thomas Jefferson in 1814 for his friend, the Governor of Virginia, James Barbour. Barbour was an important personality in the early decades of American political life, first as governor of Virginia (1811–14) and later as senator (1815–25) and member of a number of presidential commissions at least until 1839. The villa was designed to dominate the surrounding landscape. Jefferson's original plans called for a dome over the large central hexagonal space leading to the rooms for entertaining guests, but it was never built. The building was made of brick with the entrance through a large white-stuccoed colonnaded portico. The villa was damaged by a fire that broke out on Christmas day 1884. The Barbours then abandoned it and moved into two large buildings on the side of the hill to the west of the main villa. In the early 1900s, the two buildings were joined into a single unit which is still used as a residence. The area is immersed in magnificent vineyards that delineate and highlight the morphology of the area and give it a clearly recognizable identity.

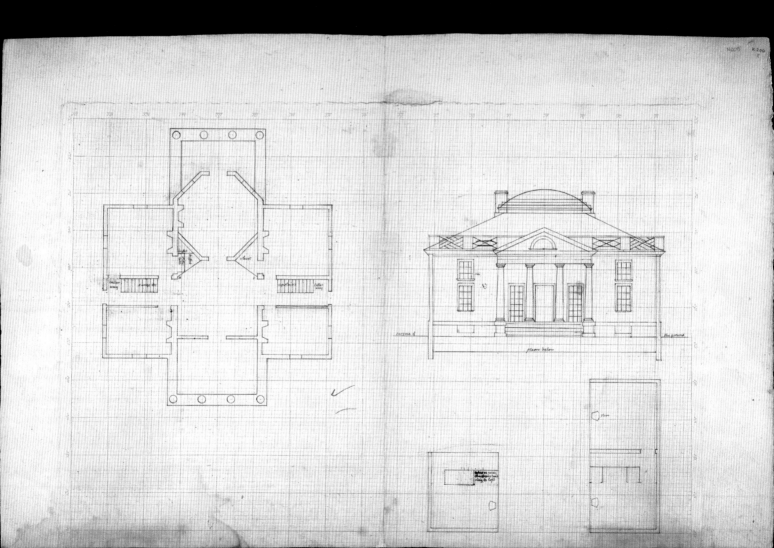

Detail of the ruins of the central octagonal hall.

BARBOURSVILLE RUINS
Historic Landmark
Designed by Thomas Jefferson
for Governor James Barbour.
Built 1814, Destroyed by Fire
Christmas Day, 1884.

Margherita Azzi Visentini*

From Palladianism to Eclecticism
The Italian Presence in the Villas and Gardens of Virginia and Washington from the Late Colonial Period to the Early Twentieth Century

* Professor, Faculty of Architecture "Bovisa", Politecnico, Milan

Italian villas and gardens have been a continuous stylistic reference point for North American private residences over the last three centuries, and Virginia and the District of Columbia are no exception—quite the contrary!

American architecture in general, and particularly that concentrated in Virginia, entered history under the name of Andrea Palladio, the famous sixteenth-century Venetian architect (1508–1580). By the early twentieth century, his influence had spread from Russia to the Atlantic coasts of North and South America thanks to the fame of his buildings but even more so to his treatise, *I Quattro Libri dell'Architettura* [Four Books on Architecture], originally published in Venice in 1570 and reprinted a number of times in their entirety or, more often than not, limited to the first one.

The first book deals with the site, the materials and the five architectonic orders, which for centuries were considered the essential grammar of architecture. The second addresses private houses in the city and in the country, palaces and villas, and represents a great novelty since the author published his own projects, given the fact, as he explains, that not many specimens of domestic architecture had survived. The third discusses public buildings, streets, and bridges, while the fourth focuses on temples and religious architecture in general.[1]

In his buildings Palladio gave a very personal interpretation of late Renaissance architectural principles, combining ancient models and harmonious proportions with a great attention to the practical and aesthetic needs of the patrons. In his villas, which are both beautiful buildings according to the late Renaissance interpretation of antiquity and functioning factories, he succeeded in meeting the demands of the Venetian ruling class, forced to convert its economy from trade to agriculture following the Turkish conquest of Constantinople (1453) and the discovery of America. One of Palladio's inventions was the "villa temple." In its center, marking the patron's private quarters, he incorporated the glorifying element of a monumental stairway going up to an open loggia or *pronaos*, crowned by a triangular frontispiece and, in a few cases, such as the Rotonda, by a dome. He also associated it with utilitarian outbuildings, symmetrically located at the two sides of the mansion and directly linked to it by means of covered passages, often in the form of open porticoes, forming a single, well conceived "body," as Palladio himself explains.[2]

Thanks to the plates included in the *Secondo Libro*, the Palladian villas and palaces became known throughout the world, even on the other side of the Atlantic. To be precise, there was no direct connection between the British colonies of North America and Venice in the eighteenth century—all came through England, the mother country.

As is well known, English architecture had a long connection with Palladio, and British Palladianism has quite a long history. All began with Inigo Jones (1573–1652), the Surveyor of the Stuart Kings, James I and Charles I, who, after the long isolation of the Elizabethan era, opened Britain to continental Renaissance culture.[3] At the beginning of

Thomas Jefferson, the front portico to the Monticello manor.

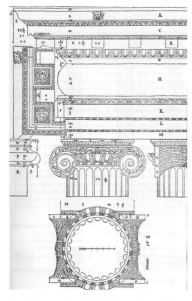

"Ionic Order," from A. Palladio, *I Quattro Libri dell'Architettura*, Venice 1570, Book 1.

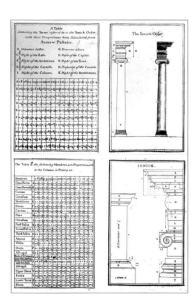

"Ionic Order," from W. Halfpenny, *Practical Architecture*, 1724.

the seventeenth century he traveled to Italy. He visited Rome, but spent most of his second sojourn in Vicenza and Venice. He bought a copy of the *Quattro Libri*, which he carried with him, recording the differences between the printed plates and the actual buildings. He met old architect Vincenzo Scamozzi (1552–1616) and purchased a great number of Palladio's drawings, which he later studied carefully. He returned to England, where he opened the way to English architectural Classicism under the name of Palladio, at the same time when Bernini and Borromini were just starting to develop the new Baroque architecture in Rome.

Jones's art did not make a wide impact in his own time, since he worked almost exclusively for the Court and realized only a few of his many ambitious projects. Moreover, his career came to an abrupt end with the first English revolution and the dramatic death of his patron, King Charles I, in 1644. He became a very important point of reference, however, for the much more popular eighteenth-century Neo-Palladianism. Political and ideological implications had a major role in the development of the new artistic movement, usually dated to 1715. In that year, two important publications appeared: Palladio's *Four Books on Architecture*, in an elegant edition published by the Venetian Giacomo Leoni, and the first book of Colen Campbell's *Vitruvius Britannicus*, a collection of one hundred views of classical English architecture in which Inigo Jones had a major part.[4] Both books were dedicated to the new king, George I of Hannover (1714–1727).

It was only when Lord Burlington became the enthusiastic patron of the Neo-Palladian movement and went to the Veneto, where he bought a great number of Palladio's drawings in addition to those purchased from Inigo Jones's heirs (thus assembling the greatest collection of drawings of the great Venetian architect), that a new, more purist interpretation of Palladio's teaching started to take form.

Eighteenth-century English Neo-Palladianism is indeed a unique phenomenon in the history of Western architecture. Due to the wisely organized campaign, the convinced support of influential patrons, a strong national pride and the increasing international prestige and wealth of Great Britain, the new style was immediately accepted among London intellectual circles. From there, in a simplified, less pretentious form, it rapidly reached even remote parts of the country and spread all over Europe and to America. There were not enough architects to satisfy the great demand, so a new kind of publication was invented. It fell somewhere between the elegant, expensive, and not-easily-interpreted folio-volume books, and the more practical and less pretentious carpenters' manuals. These books were intended to transmit the fashionable Palladian taste to the less cultivated artisans, or even to simple amateur architects who wished to renovate their homes in the new style. There were models for any financial level, from the most elegant mansions to quite small family houses.

These pattern books were often published in reduced dimensions, they were full of illustrations, and classical rules were simplified to the point that they could be understood even by "the meanest capacity."[5] The proportions of the different parts of the architectonic orders had traditionally been expressed through the relative mean of the module (a conventional unit, usually half the diameter of the column), a system that implied complicated mathematical calculations. In the new publications, they were now expressed in absolute numbers, and even translated into feet and inches. It thus became extremely simple to construct any part of a classical order correctly with the help of these pocket-books. A comparison between the Ionic order as presented in Palladio's *Quattro Libri* and that illustrated in *Practical Architecture* by William Halfpenny, printed in 1724 (and at only twelve centimeters, one of the smallest pocket-books), is very instructive. Sometimes the relationship between these books and Palladio was extremely indirect or even non-existent. Very often Palladio's name was improperly used. But the fact that they mentioned him was

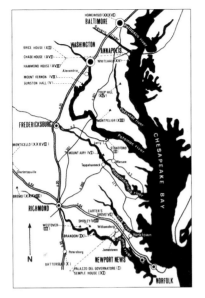

Plan of Tidewater Virginia and Maryland with the main plantation houses (from Azzi Visentini 1976, fig. 36).

enough to guarantee the success of these books, responsible for the spread of British Neo-Palladianism in England's American colonies.[6]

Between 1760 and 1820 Palladio was the most frequently mentioned architect in North America. Single elements, like doorways, windows and chimney pieces, and even complete buildings were executed in the Palladian style during the late colonial period in almost every colony, from New England to Georgia. But the style reached its fullest expression in Virginia, one of the colonies most loyal to the British crown. Virginia (and particularly, in colonial time, the Tidewater section along the Chesapeake Bay) developed economically and socially in a very peculiar way. Since it depended mainly on one single crop, tobacco, which quickly exhausted the soil so that new land was continuously required, small properties could not survive and were incorporated into large plantations. As a result, by the middle of the eighteenth century no more than one hundred families had amassed both economic and political power, forming a true landed aristocracy. The plantation, based on slave labor, formed a small social and urban community having the plantation owner as absolute legal authority, and his mansion, the largest and most pretentious building, as the core of its architectural composition. In this it mirrors Palladio's villas, composed of the elegant quarters of the masters with utilitarian outbuildings arrayed around it in a hierarchical and symmetrical arrangement. In Virginia, the mansions were located, where possible, close to one of the four major rivers (the Potomac, the Rappahannock, the York and the James) crossing the colony from west to east, from the Piedmont Mountains to the Chesapeake Bay, which emptied into the Atlantic Ocean. This arrangement allowed them to send their crops directly by sea to Bristol or London.

The new Virginia aristocrats were eager to establish their status. Their children were sent to London to attend schools and universities. Their ships, going to England laden with tobacco, returned with the latest in luxury products: clothes, *objets d'art*, furniture and books, including architectural treatises. Sometimes the shipments included entire architectural elements such as doors or chimney pieces. Obviously, everything English was fashionable, and with the private, direct ties between Virginia's richest families and the mother-country, Neo-Palladian taste reached this colony earlier than others, around 1730–40, during the so-called mid-colonial period.[7]

We now present a few examples to demonstrate Palladio's role in this phase of American architecture. Let us start with Westover, a huge plantation situated along the James River about twenty miles west of the capital, Williamsburg. It has been in the Byrd family for many generations. There, around 1730, William Byrd II (1674–1744), educated in London at Middle Temple, decided to build his new mansion. In a letter sent in 1729 to a Mr. Spencer in London, he announced that "in a year or two I intend to set about building a very good house."[8] A massive, square brick building, surmounted by a very tall roof, which is more than one-third of the total height, Westover appears, at first glance, to be a typical example of early colonial style, a provincial expression of the English Wren tradition. But a few details indicate the beginning of a new approach to architecture, such as the manifest tendency to overall symmetry, more evident in the exterior, and the two outbuildings located at either side of the mansion (they were originally separated from it), along with a number of decorative features. The house is approached from the

Westover, south front. Photo Jean Baer O'Gorman, c. 1974 (from Azzi Visentini 1976, fig. 63).

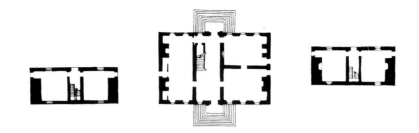

"Doorway, Composite Order," from. W. Salmon, *Palladio Londinensis*, London, 1734, Plate XXVI. Westover, doorway, south front. Photo Jean Baer O'Gorman, c. 1974 (from Azzi Visentini 1976, figs. 66 and 68).

land-side via an elegant ironwork gate, with side pilasters crowned by eagles, the king of birds, in honor of the Byrd family. But the new style is most strongly represented in the two main doorways. Carved in white Portland stone, sharply contrasting with the intense red of the brick walls, they are modeled exactly after plates XXV and XXVI of William Salmon's *Palladio Londinensis*, or *The London Art of Building*, first published in London in 1734. We do not know for certain whether they were executed in England or in the colonies. However, despite their accurate execution—something which was uncommon at the time in America—and in view of the precise reliance on a printed plate, something that an expert London stone carver would not have done, preferring to add a personal touch, colonial execution seems to be the most plausible.

On the south side, the riverfront, once the main access to the mansion, we find the elegant composite doorway, with the superimposed swan motif, so characteristic of seventeenth-century England, but something that Palladio would never have accepted. The chimney piece of the main hall was extracted from an even more pretentious source, *A Book of Architecture* by James Gibbs (1728).

Mount Airy in Richmond County, built between 1758 and 1762 for Colonel John Tayloe II, belongs to a later moment in the history of Georgian architecture in the American colonies. Tayloe's family, who reached Virginia during the first half of the seventeenth century, had accumulated a great fortune as tobacco growers and merchants, and had gained recognized social status. The three daughters married into the best Virginian families, one becoming a Carter, another a Lee, and the third a Lloyd. The mansion itself is an impressive testament to the refined tastes of its owner. Mount Airy is a very special building in a number of respects. It is situated in a picturesque and elevated position, overlooking the Rappahannock River valley to the south, where the previous old Tayloe mansion had been located before it was destroyed by fire in 1740. The use of stone as a building material was rare in Virginia, where most of the houses were built of wood or— for those who could afford it—brick. Stone was not locally available, and it was usually employed only for important details.

Unlike Westover, where just a few elements were extracted from the literature, Mount Airy, with its central mansion and outbuildings, was copied in its entirety from plates in architecture books. These were not part of the popular literature addressed to non-specialized artisans, but elegant, expensive, and sophisticated folio-volume publications, such as William Adam's *Vitruvius Scoticus* (1750) and James Gibbs's *A Book of Architecture* (1728). Haddo House in Aberdeenshire, Scotland, was the reference for the north front, while the south side, or riverfront, is clearly modeled after a residence "for a gentleman in Dorsetshire," published as Plate LVIII in Gibbs's *Book*, but reduced from nine to seven bays. The three-bay projecting central pavilion of this residence, entirely rusticated and crowned by a frontispiece, with a triple-arcaded loggia below, was reproduced identically. The central pavilion of the land-facing facade, however, has a second, Doric loggia, with pilasters and entablature where the prototype had a central, pedimented doorway delimited by simple rectangular windows. The main building, situated on a high basement in an artificially prominent position, like Palladio's villas, is linked via windowed passages to the two small symmetrical outbuildings, exactly as Palladio had done in Villa Badoer at Fratta Polesine and in many plates of his *Secondo Libro*. The two symmetrical wings, open porticoes for much of their length, appear to be arms embracing those who approach the house, as Palladio himself explains, and became very popular immediately after he invented them. Bernini himself was inspired by the "winged device" when he planned St. Peter's Square. By the eighteenth century the complete Palladian schema had become very popular in England, as exemplified by Colen Campbell's magnificent example of Houghton Hall.

Unlike most of the colonial mansions, which were usually designed by their owners, Mount Airy, with its exceptional character, the architectonic coherence linking plan and elevation, exterior and interior, seems to be the work of a professional architect and not that of a cultivated amateur. And there is a name that may perhaps be associated with it, that of one of the few architects active in Virginia at the time: John Ariss. Just back from England, Ariss advertised in the *Maryland Gazette* of May 22, 1751, his ability to "plan Buildings of all Sorts and Dimensions [...] in the neatest manner (and at cheaper rates), either of the Ancient or Modern Order of Gibbs's Architecture." We know that John Ariss resided in Richmond County from 1755 to 1762, the time of the construction of Mount Airy. However, no documents have as yet been unearthed to support the hypothesis that he actually designed the mansion.[9]

Mount Airy, 1758–62, river front. Photo Jean Baer O'Gorman, c. 1974.

Mount Airy, plan of the mansion and outbuildings.

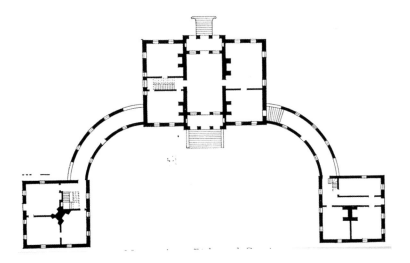

Mount Vernon, land or west front,
view of 1874.

"Venetian Window," from B. Langley, *Treasury of Designs*, 1750, Plate LI: "Model for the window of the Banqueting Hall of Mount Vernon."

Mount Vernon, north side with the Venetian window of the banqueting hall, 1773–79. Photo M. Azzi Visentini.

We move on from Mount Airy, with its sophisticated composition and well-planned design, to a more naïve and practical approach to the new Palladian fashion: Mount Vernon. The mansion, focal point of the large plantation (at the end of the eighteenth century, it included five farms and more than 8,000 acres of land) belonging to the Washington family, overlooks the Potomac River, near Alexandria, and has a long architectural history, ranging from the Early Colonial to the Federal style. Documents show that the family had originally settled there in the seventeenth century.

The irregularly-shaped original wooden cabin was in fact never destroyed. Parts of it are still recognizable under the remodeled house, a true "work in progress." George Washington (1732–1799), the first President of the United States, bought the modest family house from the widow of his elder brother, Lawrence, in 1752. He remodeled and enlarged it at different times without daring to demolish and rebuild it. We can recognize at least three building phases: 1757–58, 1773–79, and 1784–87. The first work coincides with Washington's marriage to Martha Custis and he was probably the only one responsible for the remodeling. All his efforts were addressed to giving a more pretentious classical aspect to a building originally intended only for practical purposes. He tried to ennoble the central axis of the mansion with an elegant Tuscan doorway, copied directly from a book in his library, Batty Langley's *Treasury of Designs*, first published in London in 1750. But this accentuated the otherwise irregular distribution of the openings. A new floor was added with a triangular pediment over the four central bays, to give a vague temple-front shape to the mansion. The treatment of the exterior wall is also quite interesting. Since stone was a rarity, as we mentioned above, Washington had his mansion built partly of wood and partly of brick. To give it a more pretentious aspect, however, he decided to treat the exterior beams in such a way as to imitate stone.

Between 1773 and 1779 the house was enlarged; a grand dining room was added to the left of the land entrance front, and another identical section symmetrical to it, on the right. On the side wall of the dining room a large Tuscan-Venetian window was installed. This feature was correctly executed but off-scale, too large for the wall where it was located. It, too, was copied from Langley's *Treasury*. But George Washington's Palladian ambitions went even farther. He connected the central mansion to the symmetrical outbuildings through semicircular open porches, to form a true "Palladian device." Something similar was employed, we have seen, in Mount Airy as well as in a few other late colonial mansions. A few years later, between 1784 and 1787, a severe Tuscan portico was built along the entire river front, an element more closely associated with the new Federal style than with late colonial Neo-Palladianism. The landscape around the mansion, and the general layout of his plantation, was a constant concern throughout George Washington's life. He personally conceived the famous plan drawn up by Samuel Vaughan in 1787 from a paced survey. The plan includes serpentine roads, a bowling green and wooded areas in front of the land approach to the mansion, and two distinct formal gardens at its sides, one for ornamentation and the other a kitchen garden, and well represents the transition between formal and informal design.[10]

In the meantime, the British colonies of North America had achieved independence. George Washington was of course a main figure in this delicate political and institutional transition. Another well-known Virginian, Thomas Jefferson (1743–1826), born in Albemarle County in the Piedmont region, was not only directly connected with the American Revolution, the Declaration of Independence and the birth of the United States, of which he became the third President (1801–09), but played also a major role in the history of North American architecture and landscaping.

While not a professional architect, Thomas Jefferson was far more than an amateur. His large number of architectural drawings and voluminous papers on the subject testify

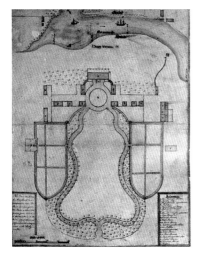

Samuel Vaughan's plan for Mount Vernon, 1787.

well to his accomplishments and many projects in the field. Later in his life he was quoted as saying: "Architecture is my delight, and putting up, and pulling down, one of my favorite amusements."[11] But his involvement with the art of building can hardly be written off as a simple "amusement." He considered architecture the most important of the fine arts, and he felt directly responsible for finding a new style that would represent the new nation, a style in which the United States could forge their own identity. In his opinion, this style had to be strictly Classical, or, more precisely, directly connected to ancient Rome, of whose literature and history he was a great admirer.[12]

His architectural ideas closely follow the history of the nation. One single building, his beloved Monticello, his residence and lifelong work, for which he chose a level-topped hill near Charlottesville in western Virginia (not far from his birthplace in the Shadwell plantation, destroyed by fire in 1770), reflects in its own genesis the entire architectural history of the country from the late 1760s to the 1820s.

There are many reasons why Monticello is one of the most significant estates in the United States. Perhaps the most important one is the identity of its patron and architect, who never ceased working on it, starting with his earliest sketches and drawings during his Williamsburg student days around 1767 and continuing for forty years or more, refining and modifying it until his death in 1826.

Its architecture is of great interest, evolving through time from late colonial Neo-Palladianism, which Jefferson would later criticize as being provincial (and of course outdated once the country had reached independence), to the neo-Classical or Federal style. Jefferson's initial house was small, only one room deep and two floors tall. It was built of brick with a front facade characterized by a double, superimposed order, Doric and Ionic, surmounted by a pediment. This element was repeated as a double loggia on the other side, where the main parlor opened onto a broad lawn. Rectangular one-floor blocks with attics were added to either side (more or less as Palladio did in Villa Cornaro at Piombino Dese). Octagonal bays would be added some time later, perhaps inspired by James Gibbs's *A Book of Architecture* (1728) and Robert Morris's *Select Architecture* (1757), both in Jefferson's library, as were a number of English editions of Palladio's *Quattro Libri*.[13] Service and storage rooms were located in symmetrical L-shaped constructions one room deep and high, running along the two sides of the mansion at basement level, leaning against the earthwork above and open toward the valley, probably a reference to the *criptoporticus* of ancient villas mentioned by Pliny the Younger and other Latin writers. But this layout, embracing on three sides the rectangular platform atop the hill, was also related to Palladio's wings, linking the utilitarian outbuildings to the main house like arms. The roofs of the L-shaped service quarters offered a panoramic terrace, running at the level of the main floor of the house with octagonal-corner pavilions.

During his stay in France from 1784 to 1789, Jefferson discovered modern French architecture (and also its ancient Roman counterpart. He said he "fell in love" with the Maison Carrée in Nîmes). He was particularly attracted to the Parisian Hôtel de Salm and to Rousseau's one-story house in the Rive Gauche, achieving a happy union of comfort and elegance. Back at Monticello, he decided to update and enlarge his mansion. He substituted the double loggias with more classical and severe large Doric temple fronts extending up two floors on either side. He added a second row of rooms toward the lawn, and a full second floor (camouflaged from the outside by joining the first- and second-floor windows, as in the Hôtel de Salm) crowned by an uninterrupted balustrade. Octagonal bays were doubled in the sides and the parlor was remodeled with a full octagonal plan surmounted by an octagonal dome. Palladio nevertheless always remained his point of reference, even though Jefferson's attention shifted from Palladio's own work, as illustrated in the *Libro Secondo*, to his interpretation of classical architecture. The *Libro Primo*, dealing with

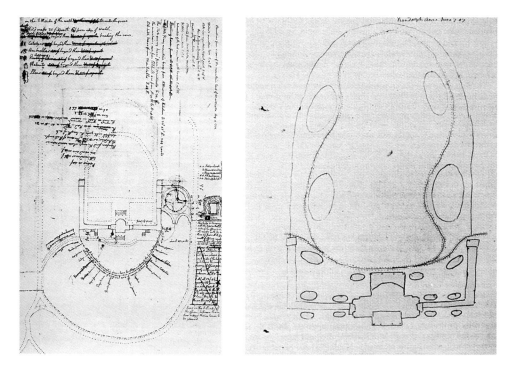

the five orders of architecture, and books three and four later became his main subjects of interest. In reference to Monticello, Jefferson explained, "The interior of the house contains specimens of all the different orders except the composite, which is not introduced. The hall is in the Ionic, the dining room is in the Doric, the parlor is in the Corinthian, and the dome is in the Attic [...] In the other rooms are introduced several different forms of those orders, all in the truest proportions according to Palladio."[14] Monticello moreover represents Jefferson's approach to private architecture, for which he admitted a free balance between tradition and innovation. The interiors, completely independent from the exteriors, had to be functional—and this is another facet of Jefferson's modern approach. Public architecture, on the other hand, had to be more severely dependent upon ancient prototypes, since it had an important representational role to play.

Monticello is also remarkable for its landscaping. During his stay in Europe, Jefferson had the opportunity to visit England and was much taken by its picturesque gardens, of which he already had some indirect knowledge. He later reworked the general layout of the grounds, moving away from the original "eclectic" landscaping with a formal section in front of the house (although we may see references to the British picturesque taste as early as 1771 in a cemetery and a spring garden, with Gothic and classic references, never built), to the later serpentine walk and oval flower beds of the central lawn, to which he dedicated great attention. The general landscaping of Monticello was a primary concern for Jefferson, who romantically located his house on a hill overlooking the Blue Ridge Mountains, with a picturesque, open view all around. And he also provided, perhaps showing some intuition about the future, an open view to the west, breaking with the tradition of colonial Tidewater mansions. With Jefferson's acquisition of the Louisiana Purchase in 1804, the west would become the new and challenging frontier for the United States. The west also contained some of the most sublime natural views, such as the Natural Bridge, some eighty miles away, which would soon become one of America's proud symbols. Jefferson carefully studied the approaches to the mansion, with four roundabouts providing the best views of the house and its natural surroundings.[15]

Monticello is extremely significant for Jefferson's vision of the future by the new country that it represents. He intended his estate to uphold an ideological approach to life, with an economic and social order grounded in a self-sufficient agricultural system, completely

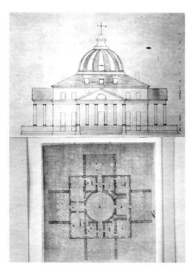

Thomas Jefferson, proposal for President's House modeled on Palladio's Rotonda, c. 1792.

different from the tobacco plantations and the slave-based production of the colonial tradition. His vision included scientific farming and new crops. He introduced vines, olive trees and rice from Italy with the collaboration of the expert Tuscan horticulturalist, Filippo Mazzei, who lived for a few years in the nearby Colle mansion. And his model differed from its city-centered, mercantile and industrial counterpart, championed by northern politicians, starting with John Adams, and which would win out in the end.[16]

During the design competition for the White House in Washington in 1792, Jefferson proposed an exact copy of Palladio's villa built for the prelate Paolo Almerico, the famous Rotonda, as it was published in the *Quattro Libri*. This building, considered the quintessence of Classical perfection, was widely imitated in Georgian England. We need remember only Colen Campbell's Mereworth Castle (1723) and Lord Burlington's Chiswick House (1724). Jefferson's design, as we know, was not accepted.

Let us now move to the outskirts of the newly founded capital of the United States. There, in 1800, construction began on the initial section of a mansion located on an estate of some 22 acres atop Georgetown hill, known today as Dumbarton Oaks. The Federal-style brick building changed ownership and appearance a number of times in the period leading up to 1920, when diplomats Robert and Mildred Bliss decided to settle in Washington after many years abroad. They purchased this Georgetown estate, asking architect Lawrence White and landscape architect Beatrix Jones Farrand to adapt the house and gardens to their tastes and needs. Their dynamic teamwork contributed to the overall success of the project, particularly the gardens, completed in 1933, which Farrand regarded as "the most deeply felt and best work in fifty years of practice."[17] The final result was a free and very personal interpretation of the Italianate tradition that dominated the United States in the first decades of the twentieth century.

At the end of the nineteenth century, with the rediscovery of the Italian Renaissance and early Baroque models by the painter, and later architect and landscape architect, Charles Platt (author of the book *Italian Gardens*, 1894) and by the novelist Edith Wharton (author of *Italian Villas and their Gardens*, 1904), a taste for formality, for a clearer, more integrated relationship of indoor and outdoor space, house and garden, began to re-

Dumbarton Oaks, aerial view. Photo Dumbarton Oaks Research Library and Art Collections, Washington, D.C.

Dumbarton Oaks, north vista.
Photo M. Azzi Visentini.

emerge. It started as a reaction to the long-lasting picturesque movement that had been flourishing for almost a hundred years since its introduction in the United States by Thomas Jefferson, through the work of Andrew Jackson Downing and up to the achievements of Frederick Law Olmsted and his circle. The new movement coincided with the so-called "Country Place Era," the result of the demand by an increased number of extremely rich patrons for bigger and more pretentious country estates, regarded as tangible symbols of their economic power. This period of American landscape architecture lasted for almost forty years, and came to an end with the Great Depression of the 1920s, the crash of 1929 and the new legislation of 1933.[18]

Raised among the most cultivated society in *fin-de-siècle* New York, Beatrix Jones, Edith Wharton's niece and later Mrs. Farrand, was encouraged to become a landscape gardener by her aunt. Beatrix helped Edith plan the Italianate gardens at her home, The Mount, in Lenox, Massachusetts in 1903–05. Beatrix completed her education at Boston's arboretum, where, under the guide of the Director Charles Sprague Sargent, she acquired a good knowledge of horticulture. The notes from her Italian travels in 1895 allow us to follow her itinerary and share in her impressions. She admired Villa Lante and Villa Aldobrandini, Castello and Boboli gardens, whose "oval basin for the fountains [...] admirably set in the oval of clipped ilex hedges [...] throw out their colors to the best advantage,"[20] was later echoed in the Ellipse at Dumbarton Oaks. In September 1895, just back from Italy, Beatrix Farrand opened her New York office and began a very successful and long-lasting career as a landscape architect.

In Dumbarton Oaks, Farrand attempted, as in all her mature works, to adjust her plan to the qualities of the place, the needs of the owners, and the use of the garden. She took freely from what she appreciated of the Western tradition, i.e., Italian formality, William Robinson's and Gertrude Jekyll's natural treatment of flower borders and beds, and some individual characteristics of American landscape architecture, which by the time had become more and more evident thanks to the potentials of its unique trees and shrubs.

The first step in planning Dumbarton Oaks was to carefully survey the topography and vegetation, which included many huge old trees. The mansion stood atop a rise sloping gently down to the south entrance, while dropping off precipitously to the north and east into the deep Rock Creek ravine. The house was to be a residence for retired diplomats who would live there throughout the year except in the summer. It would thus host large indoor and outdoor social events, but also have more intimate outdoor areas for everyday life. With these elements in mind, as well as Mrs. Bliss's declared love for evergreens and formal enclosures, Farrand proposed a series of large geometrical terraces along the back (north) and east side of the house, descending down to include cultivated fields. The problem of creating a series of gently sloping terraces descending a total of some 300 feet along the north side was particularly vexing, given the nearness of the creek to the mansion. More terraces were laid out on the east side of the house, in correspondence with the old orangery. The larger terraces were lined up freely along a central axis, from which some deviated. Others were designed as more intimate outdoor areas off to the side, initially secluded from the main view. A more irregular treatment was reserved for the areas further from the house, with a series of intermediate settings creating a smooth transition from formal to informal garden. The eastern property boundary was characterized by a natural, oval-shaped depression, indicated as a "pool" on the oldest surveying maps. This was where the Lovers' Lane pool and amphitheater were built. They were Farrand's personal interpretation of the miniature open-air theater of the Arcadian Academy in Rome, an element perfectly suited to the setting. On the northeast side, special attention was dedicated to opening long vistas, toward Rock Creek and Washington. From the north terrace one can enjoy a picturesque panorama of the capital city and the prominent minaret of the Massachusetts Avenue mosque. On the southern side of the house, Farrand decided to adopt an informal, gently winding network of paths working their way around and thus preserving the venerable old trees. The main entrance was located on this side. It was no longer considered the focal point of a rigidly biaxial composition, and thus the two fronts no longer had to match each other perfectly. New additions—the Music Room, the Byzantine Collection, the Garden Library, and the Pre-Columbian Museum (the latter two built long after Farrand's death) —were later constructed on the west side, facing 32nd Street, on the site of the old service entrance.

Stylistically speaking, Dumbarton Oaks gardens relate quite freely to the Italianate tradition. Italian gardens are anyhow to our days a main concern of the Landscape Garden Studies Department of the Dumbarton Oaks cultural institution, given to Harvard University by the Blisses themselves in 1940. The center, the last born of the three, with Pre-Columbian and Byzantine Studies, has an excellent collection of rare books, and among them many Italian published and manuscript sources, assembled by the patrons, and particularly by Mildred Bliss. Moreover, the center has always encouraged Italian studies: it was officially opened in 1971 with a memorable colloquium on *The Italian Garden* that gave new energy to the field, at the time still quite unexplored. After more than thirty years, a symposium on Italian garden studies in the last decades and on the perspectives of the field will inaugurate, in October 2007, the completely renowned architectural spaces of this world-famous institution.

[1] For the bibliography on Palladio see D. Howard, "Four Centuries of Literature on Palladio," *Journal of the Society of Architectural Historians* XXXIX, 3 (1980), pp. 224–41; L. Puppi, *Palladio. Introduzione alle Architetture e al Pensiero teorico* (Venice: Regione del Veneto and Arsenale Editrice, 2005), pp. 448–63. For a first approach: J. Ackerman, *Palladio* (Harmondsworth: Penguin Books, 1966); L. Puppi, *Andrea Palladio* (Milan: Electa, 1973; trans. by P. Sanders, London 1975; new updated edition Milan: Electa, 1999). On Palladio's treatise, see R. Pane, "I Quattro Libri", *Bollettino del Centro Internazionale di Studi di Architettura A. Palladio* [hereafter *Boll. CISA*] IX (1967), pp. 121–38; L. Magagnato, "Introduzione" to A. Palladio, *I Quattro Libri dell'architettura*, ed. by L. Magagnato and P. Marini (Milan: Il Polifilo, 1980), pp. XI-LXVI; U. Berger, "Und Palladio publiziert seine eigenen Bauten. Zur Problematik des Secondo Libro," *Architectura* 14 (1984), pp. 20–40.

[2] On Palladio's villas see G. Masson, "Palladian Villas as Rural Centers," *The Architectural Review* CXVIII, 703 (1955), pp. 17–20; J. Ackerman, *Palladio's Villas* (New York, 1967); H. Burns, *Andrea Palladio 1508–1580. The Portico and the Farmyard*, exhibition catalogue (London: The Arts Council, 1975); D. Battilotti, *Le Ville di Andrea Palladio* (Milan: Electa, 1990); M. Azzi Visentini, *La villa in Italia. Quattrocento e Cinquecento* (Milan: Electa, 1995 ff.), pp. 221–94 (with bibliography); *Andrea Palladio e la villa veneta da Petrarca a Carlo Scarpa*, ed. by H. Burns and G. Beltramini, exhibition catalogue (Venice and Marseilles, 2005).

[3] J. Lee-Milne, *The Age of Inigo Jones* (London, 1953); J. Summerson, *Inigo Jones* (Harmondsworth: Penguin Books, 1966); *The King's Arcadia: Inigo Jones and the Stuart Court*, exhibition catalogue (London, 1973); A. Cerutti Fusco, *Inigo Jones, Vitruvius Britannicus: Jones e Palladio nella cultura architettonica inglese, 1600-1740* (Rimini: Maggioli, 1985).

[4] J. Summerson, *Architecture in Britain* (Harmondsworth: Penguin Books, 1970; first ed. 1953), pp. 317–93; P. Murray, "Il Palladianesimo," in *Palladio*, exhibition catalogue (Milan, 1973), pp. 157–69; R. Wittkower, *Palladio and English Palladianism* (London: Thames and Hudson, 1974); C. M. Sicca, "Il Palladianesimo in Inghilterra," in *Palladio: La sua eredità nel mondo*, exhibition catalogue (Milan, 1980), pp. 31–71; J. Harris, *The Palladians* (London: The Trefoil Books, 1981), and *The Architect and the British Country House, 1620–1920*, exhibition catalogue (Washington, D.C., 1985), pp. 36–50, 112–51. The word "Palladianism" has been so widely and indiscriminately used in recent years to emphasize the so-called "fortune of Palladio" and "his legacy in the world," without geographical and historical borders, that it has lost meaning. See M. Kubelik, "Il Palladianesimo: Appunti critici," in *Contributi su Andrea Palladio nel Quarto Centenario della morte (1580-1980)* (Venice, 1982, pp. 91–106). There have been attempts to follow the fortune of one single element, such as J. Reynolds, *Andrea Palladio and the Winged Device* (New York: Creative Age Press, 1948). But the problem still awaits a clear answer. On Leoni's edition and on English Palladian books see R. Wittkower, "Giacomo Leoni's Edition of Palladio's 'Quattro Libri dell'Architettura'," *Arte Veneta* VIII (1954), pp. 310–16, and "Le edizioni inglesi del Palladio," *Boll. CISA* XII (1970), pp. 293–306; M. Azzi Visentini, "La fortuna del neopalladianesimo inglese e la letteratura neopalladiana 'minore'," *Comunità* 170 (October 1973), pp. 322–406; J. Dobai,

Die Kunstlitemtur des Klassizismus und der Romantik in England, I, 1700-1750 (Bern, 1974); J. Archer, *The Literature of British Domestic Architecture, 1715–1842* (Cambridge, Mass. and London: MIT Press, 1985). For a complete list of the *Quattro Libri* editions, see Magagnato and Marini 1980, pp. LXVII–LXXI. In the "Preface to the Reader" Leoni explains that he had freely corrected the plates to adapt them to the English taste so that they can be considered originals instead of just improved copies.

[5] As explained in B. and T. Langley, *The Builder's Jewel* (second ed. 1746), a book so small as to be "made fit size for the Pocket," and so simple to be understandable to those "Absolutely unacquainted with this noble Art." Azzi Visentini 1973, pp. 390–91. W. Halfpenny, B. and T. Langley, W. Salmon, F. Price, W. Pain and A. Swan are among the most prolific authors, and those most sold in the colonies, where they were also reprinted. H. R. Hitchcock, *American Architectural Books* (Minneapolis, 1962; first ed. 1946).

[6] The presence of English Palladian literature in the American colonies has been studied by H. Park, "A list of Architectural Books Available in America Before the Revolution," *Journal of the Society of Architectural Historians* XX, 3 (October 1961), pp. 115–30, and *A List of Architectural Books Available in America Before the Revolution* (Los Angeles, 1973); J. B. Schimmelmann, *Architectural Treatises and Building Handbooks Available in American Libraries and Books Stores through 1800* (Worcester, Mass., 1986). On late colonial architecture see H. D. Eberlein, *The Architecture of Colonial America* (Boston, 1915); C. Bridenbough, *Peter Harrison: First American Architect* (Chapel Hill, NC, 1949); T. T. Waterman, *The Dwellings of Colonial America* (Chapel Hill, NC, 1950); H. Morrison, *Early American Architecture from the First Colonial Settlements to the National Period* (New York, 1952), pp. 270–565; F. Kimball, *Domestic Architecture of the American Colonies and of the Early Republic* (New York, 1966; first ed. 1922), pp. 53–141; Architect's Emergency Committee, *Great Georgian Houses of America*, 2 vols. (New York, 1970; first ed. 1933–37); W. Pierson, *American Buildings and their Architects: The Colonial and Neoclassical Styles* (New York, 1970), pp. 111–56; M. Whiffen and F. Koeper, *American Architecture, I. 1607–1860* (Cambridge, Mass., 1981; first ed. 1981), pp. 76–100. On the presence of Palladio in American architecture, see J. Ackerman, "Palladio e l'architettura del '700 negli Stati Uniti," *Bollettino del Centro Internazionale di Studi di Architettura A. Palladio* VII (1964), pp. 29–38; M. Azzi Visentini, *Il palladianesimo in America e l'architettura della villa* (Milan: Il Polifilo, 1976); W. M. Whitehill and E. D. Nichols, *Palladio in America*, exhibition catalogue (Milan, 1976), pp. 99-127; H. H. Read, *Palladio's Architecture and its Influence* (New York, 1980), pp. 107–29; M. Azzi Visentini, "Palladio nell'America del Nord," *Il Veltro* XXXVI, 3–4 (May–August 1982), pp. 195–210; M. Azzi Visentini, "Palladio in America, 1760–1820," in *The Italian Presence in American Art: 1760–1860*, conference papers (New York, 1987), ed. by I. Jaffe (New York: Fordham University Press, 1989), pp. 231–49.

[7] E. S. Morgan, *Virginians at Home* (Charlottesville, 1962; first ed. 1952); L. B. Wright, *The Cultural Life of the American Colonies, 1607–1763* (New York, 1962), pp. 1–22; L. Morton, *Robert Carter of Nomini Hall* (Charlottesville, 1964; first ed. 1941); P. A. Bruce, *Social Life in Old Virginia* (New York, 1965; first ed. 1910). On private architecture and gardens in Virginia during the late-colonial and early federal periods, see A. G. Lockwood, *Gardens of Colony and State* (The Garden Club of America, 1934); T. T. Waterman, *The Mansions of Virginia, 1706–1776* (New York, 1946); T. T. Waterman and J. A. Barrows, *Domestic Colonial Architecture of Tidewater Virginia* (New York, 1969; first ed. 1932); A. Leighton, *American Gardens of the Nineteenth Century* (Amherst, 1987); P. Martin, *The Pleasure Gardens of Virginia: From Jamestown to Jefferson* (Princeton: Princeton University Press, 1991).

[8] Quoted in Waterman 1946, p. 149.

[9] Ibid., p. 244.

[10] On Mount Vernon, its gardens and landscape see N. T. Newton, *Design on the Land. The Development of Landscape Architecture* (Cambridge, Mass. and London: The Belknap Press of Harvard University Press, 1971), pp. 253–57; G. Washington, *The Diaries of George Washington*, ed. by D. Jackson and D. Twohig, 6 vols. (Charlottesville: University of Virginia Press, 1976–79); E. K. De Forest, *The Gardens and Grounds at Mount Vernon: How George Washington Planned and Planted Them* (Mount Vernon: Mount Vernon Ladies' Association of the Union, 1982); A. Leighton, *American Gardens in the Eighteenth Century. "For Use or for Delight"* (Amherst: The University of Massachusetts Press, 1986; first edition 1976), pp. 248–69; R. F. Dalzell Jr. and L. B. Dalzel, *George Washington's Mount Vernon: At Home in Revolutionary America* (New York: Oxford University Press, 1998); M. K. Griswold, *Washington's Gardens at Mount Vernon: Landscape of the Inner Man* (Boston: Houghton Mifflin, 1999); M. J. Manning, "Mount Vernon," in *Chicago Botanic Garden Encyclopedia of Gardens*, ed. by C. A. Shoemaker, 3 vols. (Chicago and London: Fitzroy Dearborn Publishers, 2001), II, pp. 918–21.

[11] See E. D. Nichols, *Thomas Jefferson's Architectural Drawings, with Commentary and a Check-List* (Charlottesville and Boston, 1961), p. 3. See also, for an inventory of Jefferson's architectural drawings (more than five hundred, preserved in different American libraries and institutions) F. Kimball, *Thomas Jefferson, Architect: Original Designs in the Collection of Thomas Jefferson Coolidge* (New York, 1968; first ed. 1916). For the writings of Jefferson see *The Writings of Thomas Jefferson*, ed. by P. L. Ford, 10 vols. (New York, 1892–99); T. Jefferson, *Notes on the State of Virginia* (1788), ed. by W. Peden (New York, 1954); A. A. Lipscomb, *The Writings of Thomas Jefferson*, 20 vols. (Washington, D.C., 1903); *The Papers of Thomas Jefferson*, ed. by J. P. Boyd (Princeton, 1950); D. Malone, *Jefferson*, 6 vols. (Boston, 1948–84). On Jefferson as an architect, see I. T. Frary, *Thomas Jefferson, Architect and Builder* (Richmond, 1931); W. B. O'Neal, *A Check-List of Writing on Thomas Jefferson as an Architect* (1959); Pierson 1970, pp. 286–333; Whiffen and Koeper 1981, pp. 100–09; *The Eye of Thomas Jefferson*, exhibition catalogue, ed. by W. H. Adams (Washington, D.C., National Gallery of Art, 1976). Monticello most probably takes its name from Palladio's description of the site, on the top of "*un monticello di ascesa facilissima*," of the Rotonda in the *Quattro Libri*, even if it is not clear where Jefferson read it, since he owned only English translations of the treatise and he did not know Italian. W. H. Adams, *Jefferson's Monticello* (New York, 1983); J. Waddel, "The First Monticello," *Journal of the Society of Architectural Historians* XLVI (1987), pp. 5–27; J. McLaughlin, *Jefferson and Monticello. The Biography of a Builder* (New York: Henry Holton and Company, 1988); J. Ackerman, *The Villa. Form and Ideology of Country Houses* (Princeton: Princeton University Press, 1990), pp. 185–211.

[12] K. Lehmann, *Thomas Jefferson, American Humanist* (New York, 1965; first ed. 1947).

[13] On Jefferson's library see E. M. Sowerby, *Catalogue of the Library of Thomas Jefferson*, 5 vols. (Washington, D.C., 1952–59); W. B. O'Neal, *Jefferson's Fine Arts Library: His Selections for the University of Virginia, Together with His Own Architectural Books* (Charlottesville, 1976). Jefferson owned Palladio's *Four Books of Architecture*, in Leoni's editions of 1715 and 1742, and he continually looked at them his life through. From Jefferson's papers it is clear that he considered Palladio's treatise a real authority. Writing in 1804 to the Virginia mason James Oldham who had asked him how to purchase a copy of the *Quattro Libri*, Jefferson explained the difficulty, "in the meantime," he added, "as you may be distressed for present use, I send you my portable edition, which I value because it is portable: you will return it at your own convenience. It contains only the 1st book on the orders, which is the essential part. The remaining books contain only plans of great buildings, temples, &c…"; Sowerby

1952–59, IV, p. 360. Later, in 1816, General John Hartwell Cocke of Bremo referred that Jefferson used to say that "Palladio was the Bible. You should get in and stick close to it"; Kimball 1968 and Azzi Visentini 1989, pp. 241–42, 246. Palladio's treatise was, together with Ronald Fréart de Chambrai's *Parallèle de l'architecture antique et la moderne*, published in Paris in 1650, the main reference for the orders, all different, copied from famous specimens of antiquity, of the pavilions of the Charlottesville campus. Among the architectural books owned by young Jefferson and studied by him were also James Gibbs's *Rules for Drawing the Several Parts of Architecture* (1728) and *A Book of Architecture* (1732), together with Robert Morris's *Select Architecture* (1757).

[14] Lehmann 1965, pp. 168–69.

[15] Jefferson visited some of England's most famous picturesque gardens in 1786. But despite his enthusiasm for the new style, which he introduced to America and in great part adopted in the plans for the grounds of Monticello, he never entirely rejected the Classical, regular tradition. W. A. Lambert and W. H. Manning, *Thomas Jefferson as an Architect and a Designer of Landscape* (Boston and New York: Houghton Mifflin, 1913; reprint 1989); S. A. Robertson, *Thomas Jefferson and the Eighteenth-Century Landscape Garden Movement in England* (Ann Arbor, 1978); F. D. Nichols and R. E. Griswold, *Thomas Jefferson, Landscape Architect* (Charlottesville: University of Virginia Press, 1978); see also Newton 1971, pp. 255, 258; W. D. Beiswnager, "The Temple in the Garden: Thomas Jefferson's Vision of the Monticello Landscape," in *British and American Gardens in the Eighteenth Century*, ed. by R. P. MacCubin and P. Martin (Williamsburg, 1984), pp. 170–88; P. J. Hatch, *The Gardens of Thomas Jefferson's Monticello* (Char-

lottesville: Thomas Jefferson Memorial Foundation, 1992); P. J. Hatch, *The Fruit and Fruit Trees of Monticello* (Charlottesville: University Press of Virginia, 1998).

[16] On Filippo Mazzei's horticultural collaboration in introducing and adapting new crops from Italy, started around 1773 and failing a few years later, see Nichols and Griswold 1978, pp. 139–42. For Jefferson's interests in horticulture and agriculture, and his plans for Monticello, thought as an American *ferme ornée*, see *Thomas Jefferson's Garden Book, 1766–1824*, ed. by E. M. Betts, Philadelphia 1944; A. W. W. Griswold, *Farming and Democracy* (New York, 1948); *Thomas Jefferson Farm Book*, ed. by E. M. Betts (Philadelphia, 1957); M. D. Peterson, *Thomas Jefferson and the New Nation: A Biography* (New York, 1970); Azzi Visentini 1976, pp. 242–44.

[17] G. Masson, *Dumbarton Oaks: A Guide to the Gardens* (Washington, D.C., 1968), p. 6. See also D. K. McGuire and L. Fern, *Beatrix Jones Farrand (1872–1959): Fifty Years of American Landscape Architecture*, VIII, Dumbarton Oaks Colloquium on the History of Landscape Architecture (Washington, D.C., 1982); D. Balmori, D. K. McGuire and E. M. McPec, *Beatrix Farrand's American Landscapes: Her Gardens and Campuses* (Sagaponack, 1985).

[18] *The Italian Garden Transplanted: Renaissance Revival Landscape Design in America, 1850–1939*, ed. by R. G. Kenworthy, exhibition catalogue (Troy, 1988); M. Azzi Visentini, "The Italian Garden in America: 1890s–1920s," in *The Italian Presence in American Art, 1860–1920*, ed. by I. Jaffe, conference papers (New York, 1989; New York: Fordham University Press, 1992), pp. 240–65.

[19] B. Jones, *Journal, MS., College of Environmental Design Documents Collection* (Berkeley: University of California, May

12, 1989). The copious documentation available (letters, photographs, drawings, and other records) touches on this spirit of cooperation as well as on every detail of the Dumbarton Oaks project, a uniquely American adaptation of the Classical Mediterranean garden which traveling Americans came to admire in the late nineteenth century and which was so eloquently described by Edith Wharton. The design of the planting follows the tradition of Gertrude Jekyll, with a palette adapted to the climate and a selection of predominantly North American tree species. Farrand would recall, late in life, that during all her career she "tried to heed Professor Sargent's advice to make the plan fit the ground and not twist the ground to fit a plan, and furthermore to study the tastes of the owners." R. W. Patterson, "Beatrix Cadwalader Jones," in M. Bliss, R. W. Patterson and L. Roper, *Beatrix Jones Farrand, 1872–1959: An Appreciation of a Great Landscape Gardener* (Washington, D.C., 1960), pp. 1–7, at 2; W. M. Whitchill, *Dumbarton Oaks: The History of a Georgetown House and Garden, 1800–1966* (Cambridge, Mass., 1967); N. B. Beatty, *The Dumbarton Oaks Garden* (Washington, D.C., 1978); S. Tamulevich, *Dumbarton Oaks. Garden into Art* (New York: The Monacelli Press, 2001).

[20] Farrand supervised the necessary adjustments to convert a private residence garden into that of a public institution. In 1941, at the request of John Thacher, first Harvard Director of Dumbarton Oaks, Farrand wrote the famous "Plant Books for Dumbarton Oaks," which give clear instructions concerning its horticultural maintenance for the following years. *Beatrix Farrand's Plant Book for Dumbarton Oaks*, ed. by D. K. McGuire (Washington, D.C., 1980).

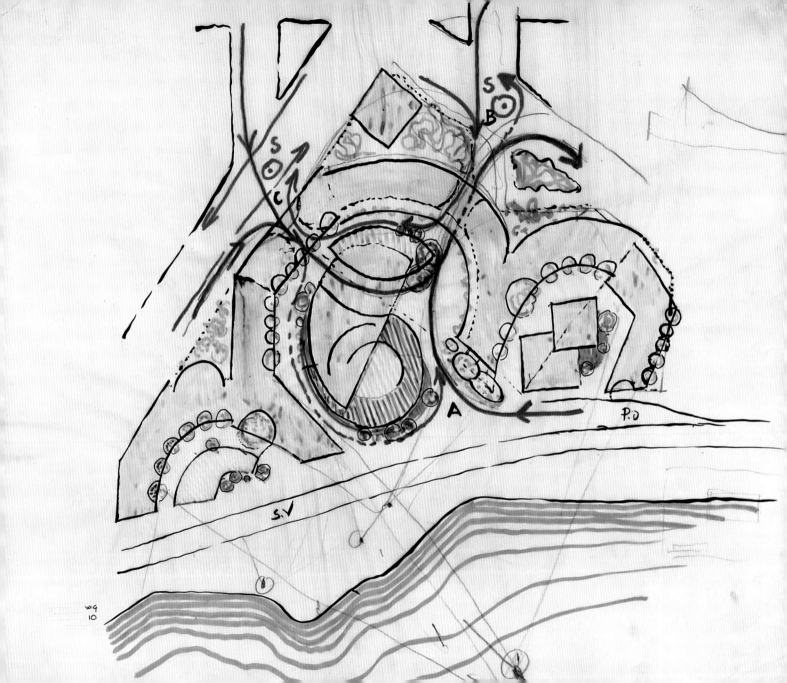

Luisa Vecchione

Interview with Giuseppe Cecchi, Developer of the Watergate Complex June 15, 2007

This interview is part of a research project titled "The American Architecture of Luigi Moretti," conducted by architect Luisa Vecchione for the 22nd cycle of the Architectural History and Criticism Doctoral Program directed by Professor Giosi Amirante at the "Luigi Vanvitelli" School of Architecture, Second University of Naples.

The Watergate Complex was developed by the Italian firm Società Generale Immobiliare, which began its activities abroad in the late 1950s. Its American affiliate, Ediltecno S.p.A., was founded in Washington, D.C. in 1961 under the direction of Giuseppe Cecchi. He chose a site along the Potomac that had been overlooked by American developers for his innovative project, based on the brilliant plans of architect Luigi Moretti. The complex was built in the 1960s on a lot adjacent to the future site of the Kennedy Center, begun in 1964, and includes offices, luxury apartments, a hotel and stores with a view of the river and the Virginia woodlands. Giuseppe Cecchi, currently president of the IDI Group, a leading construction firm, was the protagonist of this grand project. With his voice still full of youthful enthusiasm, he graciously provided an inside view of the work and spoke of his relationship with Moretti in a telephone conversation with the author.

LV. What was your job at the time?
GC. I was the manager of a company called Ediltecno, an affiliate of the Società Generale Immobiliare, and was in charge of design coordination and construction management, the technical aspects of the project.

LV. What was the situation in Washington in the 1960s?
GC. Up until 1960, you could only build commercial, office, hotel, or residential units in separately zoned areas. The city did not have a zoning for mixed-use developments. The City Council approved one in 1960 right when we were buying the Watergate site. The new zoning plan allowed mixed-use development on lots larger than 10 acres. The Watergate site was just over 10 acres and so both my firm and the Società Generale Immobiliare, accustomed in Italy to building mixed-use projects in city centers, were immediately taken by this idea and got right to work on it. The Watergate Complex was Washington's first mixed-use project; we put residential co-ops, office buildings, a hotel, and a shopping center all on the same site.

LV. The forms and curves designed by Moretti for the Watergate Complex were something new at the time for the city...
GC. Back then there was a project for the National Cultural Center just adjacent to the Watergate site. The complex was to have a theater, an opera house, and a concert hall. The architect had designed it as three circular buildings connected by circular walkways, so it was a project totally based on curves. When we met with the Planning Commission before developing our project, they told us that the design had to harmonize with the Cultural Center, and this was one of Luigi Moretti's inspirations for creating these curves. Another reason is the nature of the site along the river. Moretti wanted to embrace the green areas along the banks with his buildings. But the main reason was the Planning Commission's directive that the project should interact with the Cultural Center.

Luigi Moretti, sketch of the Watergate Complex plan.
© Archivio di Stato di Roma, Fondo Moretti.

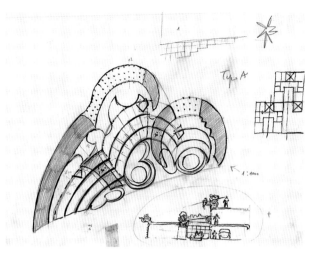

LV. ... except the Kennedy Center is rectangular.
GC. Yes. The Cultural Center plans ended up being too expensive. The funds were not available to pay for it. So they sent the architect back to the drawing board and instead of designing three circular buildings Stone conceived a rectangular building with a number of vertical columns. So the curves in the Watergate project were no longer necessary. But Moretti wanted them anyway.

LV. The Washington Post *in 1974 sharply criticized the design of the Watergate Complex. What were the impressions and reactions when the complex was completed?*
GC. Moretti's architecture was, especially then—because now the city is completely changed—very innovative and different from anything else in Washington. The city was characterized mostly by the neo-Classical architecture of all the governmental buildings, which made up the bulk of the downtown. Typical office buildings were prefabricated rectangles with precast and glass facades and the residential buildings were made of red bricks with square windows and lacked any particularly outstanding architectural features. The talented architects worked exclusively on the design of office buildings, banks, and hotels. Residential architecture was left to minor architects, who put less design effort into it. So when Moretti showed up with his highly innovative architecture there was a lot of reaction. The Fine Arts Commission really put us through the wringer. We had to go through three different agencies to get the project approved. First there was the Fine Arts Commission because they have jurisdiction over certain areas of the city—not all, but ours was one of them. Another was the Planning Commission, which was more progressively oriented and encouraged this type of architecture. And then we had to get final approval from the Zoning Commission, which was composed of three members. You see, at that time Washington did not have a mayor or a City Council. It was a federal district and was governed by three federal commissioners, who also made up the Zoning Commission. So it took us two years to get approval because the commissions all had different visions. The Planning Commission was in favor of the project, while the Fine Arts Commission was against that kind of architecture.

LV. According to Harold A. Lewis, author of the Planned Urban Development provision of the 1958 DC zoning code and one of the members of the National Capital Planning Commission, "There is no question in my mind that Watergate has a special character—that it really is unique. But I also am convinced that there is no question but that the principles of urban design and planning embodied in Watergate offer valuable lessons to cities, to developers, and to homeowners, that can be applied generally." How much influence has the

Watergate Complex had on subsequent zoning plans in the United States? What role has it played and what effects has it had on the city?

GC. Watergate was the first mixed-use project, but many more would follow. Nowadays almost every zoning district encourages mixed-use projects. It has brought innovation to the city of Washington. Previously the downtown was dead at night because it was all office buildings. And then there were the suburban residential areas that were dead during the day. But today, all cities seek to integrate functions, reduce automobile need and bring services within walking distance. Today there is a very strong thrust to design integrated mixed-use projects.

LV. Has the Watergate had any influence architecturally?

GC. In terms of urban planning it helped pave the way for the development of other multi-function buildings. In terms of architecture, there were a few attempts at imitation in a couple of buildings in the Washington area, where the architects were inspired by Moretti's example. Some adopted the continuous balconies and dentils, but the Watergate has remained a unique architectural model here in the city of Washington.

LV. Gio Ponti wrote in 1964: "This architecture by Moretti is not the 'importation' onto American soil of a modern European architect's conformist way of 'doing architecture'; it is instead the fruit of a European, an Italian, way of conceiving architecture in relation to the place, in relation to the atmosphere in which it will rise up." What is European in its design, and what is American?

GC. The construction was Americanized, but Moretti's design is totally non-American. I have never seen anything else like it in America. You might look to Gaudí for its inspiration. Moretti was a great admirer of Gaudí, he always talked about him…

LV. What was your experience working with Moretti?

GC. It was very difficult working with Luigi Moretti. Moretti designed in the Italian mode; all the plans came to us over here in meters. In Italy, architectural design was mainly an artistic expression. The architect drew up the plans and then the details of the technical systems and all the rest were worked out during construction. In the United States there was a completely different approach that demanded extreme detail. Architectural design was followed by design of mechanical systems, air conditioning, water supply, the electrical system, etc. Everything was designed down to the last rivet and screw so that everything could be perfectly coordinated, the holes could be predrilled according to designs and not done during the construction phase. So the detailed plans were drawn up by an American associate we paired up with Moretti. Moretti worked with the American architect Milton Fisher to come up with the working drawings. Naturally, the relationship between Moretti and Fisher was always difficult. Moretti designed the curves but they weren't calculated curves. He would draw them and then someone would have to see if they could be calculated. We had to use computers for this, and it was one of the first times computers were applied to construction, to make the curved panels. The first building was a sort of experiment, but the others went up really well because we had organized ourselves so we could transform Moretti's architecture into plans that could be built in America with American methods. Moretti would not allow the slightest modification to his designs, and so when he came to visit—and he came fairly often with his assistants—we always got into arguments because even though we did our best to stick to his designs, the mere fact of having to convert the measurements created the possibility of small deviations. Moretti was very rigid. He absolutely did not want any deviations from his plans and this was another difficult as-

pect of the project. In part of the ground floor the buildings are open, that is, you see the pillars. Moretti had designed these pillars in such a way that they didn't have anything to do with the interior layout of the buildings. These pillars were the fruit of the architectural composition of the ground floor, where they were visible to the eye; but then they penetrated on up through the building and in certain cases they did not correspond to the apartments layout, which had been designed without accounting for the placement of the pillars. This was a whole different [part of Moretti's design] that we had to compromise. In the first building we had to modify a great number of apartment layouts so that the pillars could go up through the building. In the other buildings this was all coordinated on the drawing board before we got the plans. It was all a very interesting experience. Moretti was a genius and created extraordinary things, and so even if it was a difficult job, in the end we managed to do it and I think that he too, when it was all finished, was very happy with the result.

LV. In October 2005, the Watergate Complex was listed on the National Register of Historic Places. In reference to Criterion C of the Register, we read: "Having had no major alterations and few minor alterations since its completion in 1971, Watergate possesses a high level of historic integrity, more than sufficient to convey, represent and contain the values and qualities for which it is significant. The property possesses a high level of integrity on all seven of the aspects of integrity required for listing in the National Register of Historic Places, including location, design, setting, materials, workmanship, feeling and association [with the political events that led to the resignation of President Richard Nixon]." How much did its political significance, in relation to the Nixon scandal, weigh in here? I mean, were the reasons for attributing historic significance to it more political or architectural?

GC. It all grew out of a dispute actually. The Watergate Complex was originally composed of three buildings of residential cooperatives (condominiums did not yet exist), a hotel, and two office buildings. The hotel was quite successful at the beginning, but in the last twenty years business was declining and the owners decided to sell it. A number of local real estate entrepreneurs put in bids for it, including myself, but my bid fell short of the selling price. Another group bought it with the intention of converting it into condominiums, but the three Watergate co-ops were opposed to having more condominiums and perhaps students from the nearby university as occupants. A rather heated dispute arose between the new hotel owners and the co-ops. In order to prevent the conversion, the co-ops pressed to have the Watergate Complex listed in the National Register of Historic Places, because in this case there are many constraints as to what you can do with it.

Luigi Moretti
Watergate Complex
Washington
1960–1971

One of the large curving residential units
looking out over the Potomac River.

Designed by the Roman architect Luigi Moretti in the period between 1960 and 1971, the Watergate Complex represents both one of the most significant and also one of the most controversial works in the recent history of Washington, D.C. Standing on the banks of the Potomac just a few blocks from the National Mall, it is one of the first truly modern buildings in a city characterized by Classical and Beaux-Arts architecture.

Built by the Italian firm Società Generale Immobiliare, the Watergate, comprising six buildings with apartments, offices, shops, and a hotel, was closely scrutinized by the authorities responsible for the architectural quality of the capital, who sought to make sure that the complex would integrate well with the city's principal urban landmarks. The result was a slow and complex process bogged down by difficult negotiations regarding heights and volumes. As a result, the Watergate Complex was not completed until 1971.

The materials used by Moretti, the variable and curving geometries making sophisticated reference to the Roman Baroque style and Moretti's earlier studies of organic forms, the variety of functions in Washington's first mixed-use project, and the richness of design all contribute to making it one of the most recognized modern monuments in the capital.

Details of the Watergate Complex.

Luca Molinari*

The Italian Chancery:
An Interview with Piero Sartogo

* Professor, Faculty of Architecture
"Luigi Vanvitelli", Naples

What was the thinking behind your approach to the project during the design contest?

Our habit is to use the architectural project as a means of interpreting the spirit of the place where the work will be built. Hence, it is essential to have an in-depth knowledge of the area and its physical and cultural context, of the setting with which the building will dialogue.

In 1992, when we were developing our conception of the project with the architects Nathalie Grenon and Susanna Nobili, we immediately realized, once we visited the site, that the area chosen for the new Chancery of the Italian Embassy in Washington, D.C. was quite relevant to the city's urban framework, and especially to the strategic area along Massachusetts Avenue, where most of the diplomatic functions are concentrated. We also noted that the Avenue has a strongly representative feel, lined as it is with some of the city's best examples of neo-Classical and Beaux-Arts residential architecture. These imposing buildings owe their allure to their general adherence to norms regarding homogeneous building height, setbacks from the road, and alignment of the facades. In addition to these morphological traits we also looked at the city plan for the new Federal capital laid out in 1791 by George Washington. The plan takes the form of a large square, 10 miles on a side, cut diagonally by the Potomac River.

What does it mean to you to build a work in Washington that represents Italy?

The thought we had in our heads was a compact building that evoked the idea of a *palazzo*, a "Euclidean" volume, pure geometry, that we would "anchor" to the site. Given that Massachusetts Avenue is one of Washington's institutional arteries and the site of many and various diplomatic offices, we had no doubt as to the need for an eminent facade that would stand parallel to the Avenue as an integral part of the urban scene. However, it was also clear that the entrance had to be off the side street. When we went onto Whitehaven Street, there were two things that caught our eye. One was the view through the Brazilian Embassy opening onto Massachusetts Avenue. The other, on the far side of Rock Creek Park, was the Washington Monument, standing as a vertical axis with respect to Whitehaven Street.

So we designed a square layout for the Chancery just like the original city plan laid out by George Washington. A diagonal cut divides the square, creating a sort of "passage" cleaving the cubic volume of the building. At one end we have a view onto Massachusetts Avenue, and at the other, of the Washington Monument. The "passage" between the two triangular volumes is a space lined by glass walls that traverses the Chancery to project itself into the park and into the city.

To conclude, I would point out that we are not dealing with a perfect square that can be inscribed in a circle. If anything, it is a decomposed figure; the square that provides the underlying inspiration for this project has undergone a number of distortions caused by its placement on the site. This square generates asymmetry.

The Italian Chancery, Washington, detail
of the main facade.
Photo: Archivio S.A.A.

The large copper door is centered with respect to the building but asymmetrical within the facade.
Photo: Archivio S.A.A.

The project area is a wooded spot next to Rock Creek Park, on Whitehaven Street not far from the intersection with Massachusetts Avenue. West of Sixteenth Street, the Avenue has a quite characteristic look, boasting some of the city's finest examples of neo-Classical and Beaux-Arts residential architecture. These impressive buildings, many of which are now diplomatic facilities, owe their charm partially to their homogeneous adherence to criteria of height, even spacing, and set-back from and alignment with the Avenue.

1. Embassy of the United Kingdom of Great Britain and Northern Ireland
2. Residential facilities for British diplomats
3. Residential facilities for Brazilian diplomats
4. Brazilian Embassy
5. The new Italian Chancery
6. Center for Hellenic Studies
7. Islamic Center.

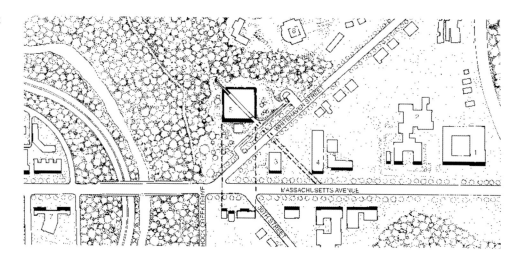

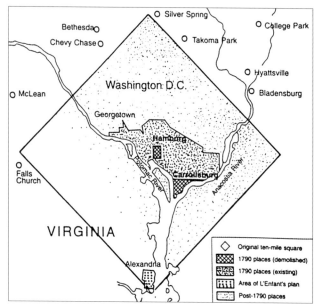

The square assumes the dimensions of two triangles, and the compact mass of the external perimeter is sliced by a diagonal. Just as the Potomac divides Washington, the glassed-in artery is a passage, a cavity, a path that slices open the building, lightening it, allowing it to dialogue with its surroundings, illuminating it, and giving order to the street–piazza–courtyard–garden sequence.

This geometry allowed us to align the main facade in the traditional manner parallel to Massachusetts Avenue while also creating a perceptual transparency, a sort of void that cuts across the building. This geometric layout was then distorted in subtle ways. The entire building is a complex of variations on the themes of the rectangle and the square. Notice for example the symmetry and proportions of the large ceremonial doorway facing onto the Avenue, placed along the axis of symmetry of the south side of the building and symmetrically within the facade containing it.

In a certain sense, what counts in the Chancery are the anomalies. They are what give it its enduring allure. For example, each facade is different; each one represents an arrangement of counterbalanced openings dug deep into a flat surface. And not all the facades are perpendicular to the ground. The one facing the woods and the steep slope of Rock Creek leans outwards as a sort of counterpoint to the natural embankment.

The broad slash that cuts through the building is just a bit off center in order to give a slight feeling of instability to the overall *mise en scène*. And in order to accentuate the sensational effect of the diagonal cut, we introduced a scheme of forced perspectives into the inner courtyard and also, with greater dramatic effect, into the alignment of the rooftops. These prow-shaped roofs, with their stepped copper rain gutters, are also different from one another. They are not all parallel, not all at the same level, but they crown the building in a stunning way with the powerful shadows they cast on the walls and their strong contrast with the sky.

How did you approach the work after you had won the design contest?
The contest process was particularly effective and as a consequence the project remained substantially unchanged in its essence during the construction phase. In this regard, the winning factor was our in-depth knowledge of structural systems and the building codes applied in the United States, where we had already done other works.

The main facade is aligned with Massachusetts Avenue as demanded by tradition. The cubic volume of the building is sliced along a north-south diagonal from Whitehaven Street to Rock Creek Park. A glassed-in space is created between the two triangular volumes that cuts across the Chancery and projects one way into the city and the other into the park.

Ground-floor plan with indication of the secant entrance plane, the large ceremonial entrance, and the glass wall at the visitor entrance.

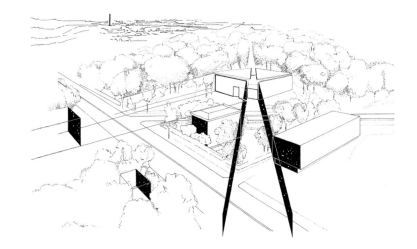

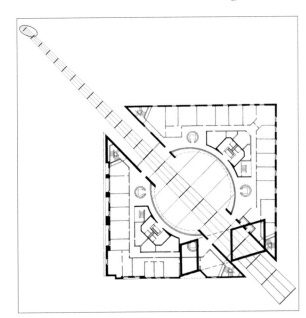

One of the elements in our approach to design is the removal of a portion excavated into the theoretical volume of the building as a means of connecting it to its urban or landscape context. The Chancery also intermixes elements of culture and historical memory, a condensation of the *forma urbis* exemplified by the designed void and urban cavities.

How does the new Italian Chancery fit into your own development?
Together with the church of the Santo Volto di Gesù, recently completed in Rome, the Chancery is one of our recent works that best exemplifies the modus operandi in architectural design that we have been developing over time, based on the principle that buildings are not ready-mades, they are not multi-purpose, interchangeable objects that can be plopped down just anywhere. On the contrary, they are site-specific works that belong to and interpret the natural or artificial landscape with which they interact. This concept of an open-ended composition is the result of years of work on the genesis of the city. In the current phase of our work, it has become our most important focus of attention and experimentation. From the building to the city, from architectural plans to urban design, this is the two-way path—still a work in progress—that describes my history.

The Chancery is a work that represents itself well externally while concentrating much of its qualities in the large roofed inner court and in its relationship to the grounds surrounding it. How do you see it functioning? What sort of scenario had you imagined, and what did you see after the work was completed?
The building is conceived to be like the human body. On the outside it has a uniform, monochromatic skin. Inside, on the other hand, it is vivaciously colored, just like our own pulsating viscera. Precisely for this difference of image…

The exterior has a solemn and institutional aspect. The walls of the four sides, all differing from one another, are characterized essentially by the choice of face-work in pink Asiago stone, with large slabs that highlight the typically Italian artisanal skill of treating stone in a tectonic manner.

These architectural characteristics underline the functions of the building: to represent, with its imposing stature, the diplomatic seat; and to allow multi-purpose use in the large central area on the ground floor, which becomes a bona fide piazza.

The stone edge continues in the copper roof.

Right from the start, we imagined the concept of this central space with its centripetal perimeter arrangements extending outwards into the grounds as an area that is open also to the external community and that in addition to fulfilling its function as a representational site can also host activities promoting the image of Italy through exhibitions, concerts, and other cultural events.

Our intuitions were borne out with time. However, I should point out that the building's first great triumph came in 1999 when the President of the American Institute of Arts, passing by the work site, asked if he could visit it, and immediately decided to hold the Architectural Awards ceremony there, in spite of the fact that work had not yet been completed. I was invited to present the Award before over 400 American architects and then, one year later, to receive it.

After this initial and very positive impact, the Chancery acquired full citizenship among the historical monuments in Washington that tell the story of the birth of the nation to the Americans, while also saying something about Italian culture and skill.

Gregory K. Hunt

The Italian Chancery: An Interview with Leo A. Daly

Mr. Daly—Italy and the United States have a long and distinguished history of exchange in culture and the arts. Before we discuss collaborations such as the one that took place on the design and construction of the new Chancery in Washington, D.C., do you have any personal remembrances of Italian culture that you would like to share with us? Has your own knowledge of Italian culture and the arts shaped your life as an architect and patron of the arts?*

This is a very interesting question and one that we should really be discussing over a 1997 vintage Brunello di Montalcino! From Federico Fellini's insightful films and the drama of Verdi's operas to the artistic experiments of the Venice Biennale and the recent architectural exhibits in the Palazzo Grassi, our two countries have shared a great deal through cultural and artistic exchange. Italy's influence on the creative arts in the United States has been both consistent and significant and its art, design and music have always been an integral part of my life as both a student and as a professional.

For instance, my early days as an architecture student at The Catholic University of America introduced me to the many famous buildings designed by Bernini, Michelangelo, Borromini, and many others—structures I always like to re-visit whenever I return to Italy, which I do frequently. Even Carlo Scarpa and Renzo Piano—architects whose remarkable sensibilities are admired by so many of us today—remain inspiring practitioners for design professionals around the world.

My own reference library of books on the subjects of art, architecture and design attests to the major contributions that Italian publishers such as Skira, Rizzoli and Electa have made to the production of so many volumes with extraordinarily high levels of content and graphic quality.

For years, my latest issue of *Domus* would always inform me of the latest design work being produced in both Italy and Europe, and it still remains the paradigm for an international publication on architecture and design. To this day, Italian furniture, fabrics, fashion, and product design consistently demonstrate Italy's high standards for design excellence.

One of my fondest remembrances was the five years I spent working with the Holy Father, Pope John Paul II, as architect of the Pope John Paul II Cultural Center in Washington, D.C. Over these years, my trips to the Vatican always left me fully inspired by this tireless advocate for world peace and harmony. Discussing the building's design with the Holy Father was always highly stimulating and his attentiveness and clarity of thought was nothing short of remarkable. I will always treasure these times of direct exchange with this extraordinary Church leader.

How did you first become involved with the new Chancery?

I first met President Francesco Cossiga at a dinner hosted by The Catholic University of America in Chicago in January 1992. The purpose of the dinner was to present the Cardinal Gibbon's medal to President Cossiga. My father and I both have served on the Board

* First question posed by Ambassador Castellaneta

of Trustees of The Catholic University of America together with the American Cardinals of the Church.

During our conversation that evening, President Cossiga informed me that Italy had outgrown its Embassy at Sixteenth and Fuller Streets in downtown Washington, D.C. and that the Italian Ministry of Foreign Affairs was considering the construction of a new Chancery on a site along "Embassy Row"—the prestigious section of Massachusetts Avenue bordered by numerous embassies and chanceries including the LEO A DALY designed Brazilian Chancery.

As a neighboring resident and an architect whose firm had been involved with many such projects for foreign countries, I discussed the nature of the site and the complexities of building in the nation's capital because of the complicated approval process. I remember it being a very stimulating conversation—President Cossiga was very conversant in architecture and design in general. Italy's many important contributions to art and architecture throughout history have always impressed me, and it was clear that he wished to have this legacy continued in the design of this new building.

How was LEO A DALY chosen to be the Executive Architect and Engineer for the new Chancery?
Our firm's extensive experience in the design and construction of U.S. embassies and foreign missions was clearly a very important factor in our being selected. Over the years we have worked with a number of foreign governments, and we knew that our comprehensive knowledge of American building practices would be of great advantage to the Ministry. It is also important to note that we are very familiar with the complex building and zoning regulations as well as the intricate approval processes in Washington, and we knew we could effectively assist the Ministry as the project went before the many agencies that would have to review the design. Personally, I was obviously highly interested in having the best possible design for a new Chancery on our block and in our neighborhood. The appreciation of the Italian Chancery has been sustained by the excellent relations with the neighbors fostered by Ambassador Castelleneta.

Because the new Chancery would represent the Republic of Italy in the capital city of the United States, the Foreign Ministry chose to organize an invited design competition in-

volving Italy's major architects. Did you feel that this competition process was the best way to select the building's architect?

I have always felt that design competitions, in general, have the disadvantage of not permitting the architect to have direct and ongoing communication with the client in the earliest phase of the design. However, for such a symbolically important and high-profiled building in Washington, D.C. the idea of selecting a design through such a competition process was, I felt, appropriate—especially because of the very comprehensive Design Guidelines that were prepared for the competitors. Because the leading Italian architects of the day were invited to participate, the Ministry chose a process that would enable the Director and others to see a variety of excellent design solutions from the best of Italy's architects. Having a number of different solutions by such talented designers would also bring forth new design ideas and architectural possibilities for consideration.

What was LEO A DALY's role in this project?

Initially, we worked for a year with Ambassador Boris Biancheri to map out the entire building process for the Chancery. We were also asked to manage the design competition. This process involved creating the set of strict Design Guidelines, that included: the preparation of full cartographic and photographic documentation of the wooded five-acre site; a detailed site analysis; a review and summary of all local building codes and zoning regulations; an outline of Washington's complex project-approval process; and information concerning all government, regulatory, and civic organizations with an influence on the project. We also conducted extensive interviews with Ministry personnel to determine internal adjacency requirements and to develop the building program and a number of diagrammatic arrangements that would enable the competition participants to satisfy the functional needs of the Embassy personnel and the staff of the Military Attache. Our responsibilities included developing phasing schedules and budget parameters for the project, and we converted all specifications into metric measurements for the Italian competitors. It was a very thorough process. During the construction phase, we worked closely with Ambassador Ferdinando Salleo who had been Director General of the Ministry of Foreign Affairs during the design process, which resulted in a seamless transition of decision-making by our client.

LEO A DALY then reviewed each competition entry with Ambassador Biancheri and his staff and made recommendations based on the various design concepts, noting their functional organizations and compliance with the Design Guidelines created by our firm.

After the proposal submitted by Sartogo Architetti Associati of Rome was selected as the winning design, we worked very closely with Piero Sartogo to develop the design. Because we were serving as Executive Architect and Engineer for the project, we had to take the initial competition design and make it reality through all the different phases, from schematic design and design development to construction documents and construction administration. We had to work out all the design details so that they would meet American construction standards, codes and regulations. I remember that the structural engineering on the project, which we did with our in-house personnel, turned out to be quite challenging.

Our office was further responsible for securing all necessary permits and agency approvals, including those from the U.S. Department of State's Foreign Building's Office (which oversees all embassy/chancery development in Washington, D.C.), the U.S. Commission on Fine Arts, the National Capital Planning Commission and the National Park Service, among others.

Do you think the Chancery's design responds sensitively to its site?

During the competition selection process, we were particularly impressed that, as an architect, Piero is always very aware of the *genius loci*, or the spirit of the place where he builds.

His design—a square building split on the diagonal by a powerful spatial axis—relates directly to the geometry of the city and to the L'Enfant Plan. This is a very subtle reference to the city as a whole. Because the square is rotated on its site so that one main elevation—the most ceremonial facade—is set parallel to Massachusetts Avenue, it faces this main urban boulevard frontally while presenting only its northern corner to the neighbors on Whitehaven Street. Great efforts were extended to save as many trees on the site as was possible. With regard to the building's overall scale, it is a four-story structure that has generous setbacks from the adjacent streets and sits very proudly—and I think very comfortably—on its site.

Do you feel that the design conveys any Italian architectural traditions?
Yes, very much so. In its form and massing, the Chancery evokes the large villas of Tuscany and even Renaissance *palazzi*—but it does so without resorting to pastiche and other Postmodern architectural devices. There is a wonderful elegance to the resolutely cubic stance the building takes in its landscape, and the elegant sloped copper roof overhang is an impressive contemporary interpretation of the traditional Italian roof cornice found in *palazzi*. One might even suggest that the ellipse of the shallow glass dome over the interior atrium subtly references a popular geometric shape used in Italian planning and architecture of the Baroque period. Inside, the use of rose-toned encaustic plaster finishes showcases the Italian mastery of material craftsmanship, as does the *Veneziana* paving patterns used both inside and outside.

Your firm also served as Engineer for this project. Did you encounter any significant engineering challenges with the design?
Above-grade, the building is of composite steel and concrete slab construction. With the introduction of the diagonal axis and the circular atrium at its center, it was structurally divided into two large triangles. This meant that the beam-to-girder steel connections at the diagonals varied, as did the beam lengths. The diagonal void through the building also meant that horizontal wind loads acting on the exterior faces of the triangles had to be transferred across this void to provide sufficient resistance to these lateral loads—and we solved the problem by designing the two bridges that cross the void as structural diaphragms capable of transferring these horizontal forces from one side to the other. The elevator cores also assist in this bracing process.

I remember that our engineers found the structure of the shallow domed skylight over the atrium to be quite complicated and structurally challenging. Due to the dome's low slope, the skylight framing introduced horizontal forces that placed the perimeter beams in torsion, and these forces had to be resolved within the steel lattice work of the framing. Finally, the complex slopes of the building's main roof meant that the elevations of each steel joist roof member had to be precisely calculated for the contractor to achieve the desired roof and cornice profiles.

With all of today's very sophisticated computer modeling, it is really interesting to note that during the building's design, we did not have advanced software such as Building Information Modeling (BIM) and other such programs to assist us with the structural calculations and detailing. In fact, most of the construction drawings for this project were done by hand!

Were there any construction difficulties with the project?
Well, yes, and all good buildings seem to have them. I recall, for example, that as we began to drill the caissons for the foundations, we discovered that the site was originally a series of gullies that drained into Rock Creek. When Massachusetts Avenue was constructed, many large trees—some over four feet in diameter—were cut down, rolled into the gullies and covered with earth. Unfortunately, these trees were not found during the geo-technical inves-

Installing the central glass roof.
Photo: Leo A. Daly Archive.

tigation and they had to be removed in order to proceed with the foundations.

I have already alluded to the complexities of the structural steel frame, which required longer fabrication time and many special connections during the erection of the steel. Similarly, the construction of the low-sloped glass dome and the fabrication of the glass itself required a number of detailed drawings, as each piece was a custom size and shape. The Italian stone used on the exterior building facades—some 42,000 pieces of "Pietra Rosa di Asiago," a soft marble—was cut and dressed in Italy, shipped to the U.S. and installed by Italian masons. Because of the restricted color range selected, many pieces of this stone had to be rejected in order to meet the tight specifications.

It is important to mention that the Chancery was constructed by a joint venture involving Beacon Skanska Construction Company of Boston, Massachusetts and Dioguardi S.p.A. of Bari (Italy). A total of 39 different firms in the United States and Italy served as subcontractors, requiring very careful coordination between the two countries during each phase of the design and construction process.

How would you summarize the quality of construction?
The new Chancery is very well constructed and beautifully crafted. From the installation of the exterior stone work and the copper roof eaves to the fabrication of the glass skylight and the laying of the *Veneziana* paving both inside and outside, the attention to quality construction and craft is immediately evident to the visitor and is a source of pride for all who work in the building.

As a resident of this neighborhood, do you feel the Chancery makes a positive addition to this portion of Embassy Row?
I feel that the Chancery relates well to the residential scale of its neighboring buildings. The sensitive site plan utilizes the dense woods to the rear as an effective natural backdrop for the building and maintains the character of the adjacent Rock Creek Park. The bucolic setting to the rear remains undisturbed and continues to be one of the neighborhood's most prized natural assets. The building was—and is—well received by my neighbors and I am proud of that fact. It is considered one of the best of Washington's contemporary structures.

Is there any one aspect of your firm's work on this significant project that you are most proud of?
The role of Executive Architect and Engineer in a project such as the new Chancery is a very important one. Working with the competition winning concept by a talented architect such as Piero Sartogo is always a great pleasure, because it requires extensive dialogue, builds on the design talents of many, and necessitates high levels of effective collaboration.

The new Chancery was a collaborative effort resulting in the construction of a very significant new edifice in our nation's capital. It is a building that unquestionably continues Italy's many contributions to contemporary architecture and the arts around the world, and I am very proud that our firm was able to assist the Republic of Italy in making yet another important addition to the built environment of Washington, D.C.

The outcome of an invitation-only design contest held in 1992 and won by Piero Sartogo and Nathalie Grenon of the Sartogo Architetti Associati studio, with Leo A Daly as executive architect, the new Chancery of the Italian Embassy in Washington has become one of the new landmarks along Massachusetts Avenue, the main locus of embassies and consulates in the American capital.

The project is based on a clear design that coherently organizes the overall spaces, the architectural grammar, and the interior layout. The desire to give form to a representative building that is both visible from the street and also an interpretation of George Washington's plan for the city inspired the designers to work with the theme of the square as a generative matrix and with the cube as a building form.

The result is a building with a monumental external aspect, with its facades built in different ways according to prospect. Great attention was dedicated to the quality of the collective and representational internal spaces. A diagonal slice divides the cube into two triangles and creates a large glass-roofed central piazza. The slice opens the cube to the outside and opens a dialogue between the central piazza and the surrounding parks and cityscape, generating a dynamic tension between interior and exterior of the new building. The interiors were conceived as a manifesto of Italian design and the Italian artisanal talent of giving form and quality to any inhabited space.

*John E. Ziolkowski**

Washington and (Ancient) Rome

* *Professor, George Washington University*

The beauty of Washington, D.C., can be credited to several influences, not least of which is the fact that the inspiration for its federal architecture derives from Classical antiquity. When plans for the new "Federal City of Washington" were being considered in the late eighteenth century, it seemed natural to follow the European tradition of designing the facades of public buildings to resemble Classical temples. The popularity of this style was based on the admiration felt for the accomplishments of the Greeks and Romans, the notion that America was in some sense a revival of their greatest aspirations in democratic republican government, and a desire to build a capital city that would impress the world with its internationally recognized symbols of "the glory that was Greece and the grandeur that was Rome."

L'Enfant's Plan

The city-plan itself was unique. It was due to the genius of the French military designer Pierre Charles L'Enfant, who first came to this country in 1776 as a young volunteer in the American cause for Independence. A few years after the war, President George Washington commissioned L'Enfant to make some drawings of the area which had been chosen for the new capital on the Potomac and identify favorable sites for public buildings. He quickly determined that Jenkins' Hill was the appropriate spot for the Congress House ("a pedestal waiting for a monument") and within the next four months proceeded to draw up his first draft that contained the principal ingredients of his final plan (1791): a chessboard pattern of streets interrupted by an irregular network of diagonal avenues and circles. Its source is not exactly known, but it is clear that no single city that he consulted offered L'Enfant the idea ready-made. On April 4, 1791, he wrote to Thomas Jefferson asking for maps of Amsterdam, Florence, London, Madrid, Naples, Paris, and Venice in order to have a variety of schemes for consideration. A few days later Jefferson sent from his personal collection maps of several of these cities plus others, but a comparison of these maps reveals that they supplied L'Enfant with only isolated suggestions for his design. The Mall, for example, was probably influenced by the Garden of the Tuileries and the gardens at Versailles, but the unique feature—radiating avenues—was not on any map of Europe. (Contrary to what might be supposed from its present appearance, Paris did not yet have a radial pattern of streets, which was created much later in the nineteenth century.) Of course the gardens at Versailles did feature radiating paths, and the American towns of Williamsburg and Annapolis had isolated examples of streets leading to traffic circles. Two plans in particular (those of Williamsburg and Versailles) illustrate similar positions for important buildings at two points of a right triangle as later proposed by L'Enfant for the President's House and Congress.

Given the predisposition for things Roman, one may wonder why a city-plan for Rome was neither requested by L'Enfant nor suggested by Jefferson, especially since the name of the Congress House was soon changed to "Capitol." This may have been because of lack of

The Washington Monument as seen through two columns of the Lincoln Memorial. Photo: Archivio Skira.

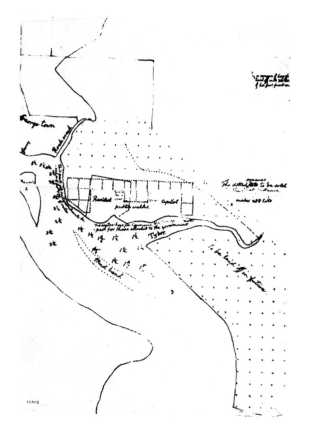

knowledge about the appearance of ancient Rome at that time, or the close identity of
Rome with the Vatican, or simply because a map of current Rome was not available. Nevertheless, a map of contemporary Rome would have provided an impressive example of
"tridentine" streets leading from the Piazza del Popolo at the northern entrance to the city.
The familiar story of the man named "Pope" who at one time owned a farm in the area
of Washington's Capitol Hill which he called "Rome" with a "Tyber" River running
through it (Goose Creek) is another indication of the predilection for identifying things here
with Roman names. Pennsylvania Avenue was sometimes referred to as Washington's "Via
Appia" in old newspaper articles. It defines the northern boundary of the Federal Triangle, which houses the federal bureaucracy in nine buildings constructed in the 1930s "in
a design reminiscent of ancient Rome."

The naming of the principal building is nevertheless somewhat curious. L'Enfant's
plan of 1791 shows "Congress House" on the map and references to this building appear
three times in the margin as "Federal House." But on Andrew Ellicott's Plan a year later
the building is designated "Capitol." Why was the name changed? It might be assumed that
the name was chosen because that was the name of its Roman counterpart and precedent.
(In the same tradition, much of our governmental terminology derives from Latin: senate,
republic, congress, legislator, election, candidate, vote, veto, etc.) But the Roman Senate
normally met in a building called "Curia" and it looked nothing like our Capitol. Sometimes the Roman Senate met in other places, particularly temples, including the Capitolium dedicated to Jupiter, Juno, and Minerva, situated on the Capitoline Hill overlooking
the Forum. According to Roman tradition the name derived from the discovery of a human head (*caput*) found in digging the foundations of the temple. In this country the usual name for the headquarters of the legislative body of each state was "State House." Other countries used different names: House of Commons, Chamber of Deputies, Parliament,
etc. Virginia was the only American State which called its main meeting place "Capitol"
when the national building was being planned. The usage goes back at least as far as 1699,

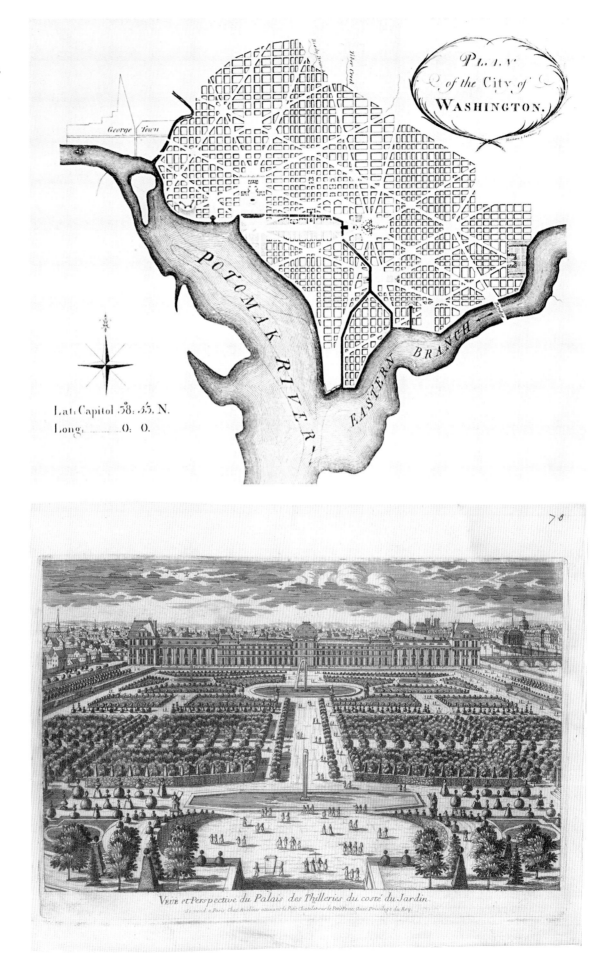

when the British passed an act directing the building of the "Capitolie and the city of Williamsburg." Thus the term was used in Williamsburg from an early date and when the seat of government was moved to Richmond in 1780, the name was naturally transferred to the new building erected there. The Federal City then was actually the third city in this country to designate its principal building in this fashion and this came about undoubtedly through the influence of Thomas Jefferson, who already had used the term on his own sketched plans for the city in 1791. Presumably by the time of Ellicott's official survey-map Jefferson's terminology prevailed as it did also in the change from L'Enfant's "Presidential Palace" to the less pompous "President's House."

It may be observed also that although the Capitol in Williamsburg was not placed on a hill top, the Capitols of Richmond and Washington were, and after that a lofty location was considered desirable for later applications in other States. This also is reminiscent of the Roman temple on the Capitoline Hill in contrast to the "Curia" (where the Roman Senate normally met), which was in the valley of the Forum. Still the question remains—why was the meeting house of Congress identified with a temple rather than the Roman Senate House? Two answers may be considered. One is that the term "Curia" (meeting-place for the "curiae" or districts of ancient Rome) had already been taken over by the Catholic Church for its central administrative body and therefore was inappropriate. The other has to do with a misunderstanding about where the Roman Senate normally met, as may be found in Shakespeare's historical plays, e.g., *Julius Caesar*:

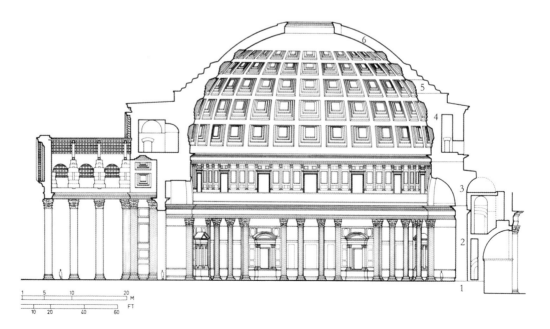

The U.S. National Capitol from the east (front).
Photo: Archivio Skira.

Cicero: "Comes Caesar to the Capitol tomorrow?" (1.3)

. . .

Decius: "Good morrow, worthy Caesar. I come to fetch you to the Senate-house." (2.2)
Plutarch and Suetonius both tell us that Caesar was killed in a meeting
of the Senate held in the *Curia Pompei*, after which his assassins marched
up to the temple on the Capitoline Hill.

The National Capitol

It is ironic that in a country whose constitution assumes the principle of the separation
of Church and State our National Capitol should be a building whose original *design* is
based on one ancient Roman temple (the Pantheon), whose *name* is that of another (the
Capitolium), and whose *modern appearance* is most like that of a Baroque church
that has been adorned by a series of Popes endeavoring to create a symbol of their power, prestige and influence in this world (St. Peter's Cathedral). The original design that
was selected for the "Congress House" (by William Thornton, 1793) had a central dome
based on the Roman Pantheon. The similarity is due not only to the general relationship
of a pedimental portico with a low dome behind it, but also to specific details: the eight
Corinthian columns and the six low stepped rings around the base of the dome. Thornton's design even indicates an "oculus" recalling the open hole in the dome of the Pantheon. This resemblance is no longer evident since the present dome is a later addition
(completed in 1863) designed by Thomas U. Walter and made of cast iron painted to look
like marble. Many artistic adornments inside and outside attest to the richness of the
early Classical influence.

The sculptural design in the central pediment is important because it set the pattern
for all the other pedimental sculptures in Washington. The nine-foot-tall figures were ex-

ecuted by Luigi Persico after a design selected by President John Quincy Adams (1825). Entitled *The Genius of America*, it consists of a figure representing *America* in the center, whose right arm rests on a shield supported by a pedestal bearing the inscription, "July 4, 1776," and her left hand points to the figure of *Justice* (identified by scales and a scroll inscribed "Constitution, 17 September, 1787"). On the left of *America* is the eagle and a figure of *Hope* resting on her anchor. The scene is intended to convey the message that as long as we cultivate justice we may hope for success.

The selection of allegorical scenes for sculptural compositions like this indicates that mythical, Christian or historical scenes were considered inappropriate for such decorations. President Adams had specifically rejected "all allusions to heathen mythology;" moreover, the location provided an opportunity for artists both to express national ideals and to allude to the specific function intended for the federal buildings. Thus neo-Classical allegory offered a compromise combining some of the recognizable vocabulary of Classical mythology, the idealism of a lofty concept, and the realism of many details. Over the other entrances to the Capitol, as well as on the other sculptural pediments (twenty-seven total) now existing on nine public buildings in Washington (on Capitol Hill, the Federal Triangle and the Mall) this practice has been followed. In this American context many Roman motifs are incorporated within the sculptural adornment: fasces, numerals, togas, Roman soldiers, oak crowns, olive branches, wreaths, and freedom caps. These lavish architectural decorations truly give the capital city a Classical appearance.

Similarly, on the national motto, as well as on those of several States, Latin phrases from Virgil and elsewhere abound: "Novus ordo seclorum," "Annuit coeptis," "E pluribus unum," "Sic semper tyrannis." As one final example from the Capitol let us examine briefly the extraordinary scene painted by Constantino Brumidi on the cupola under the dome (*The Apotheosis of George Washington*). As you enter the central entrance to the building you pass by Persico's statues of a Roman soldier representing *War* (on the right of the door) and a woman as *Ceres* or *Peace* (on the left). Then you emerge into the central chamber through a doorway decorated (by Antonio Capellano in 1827) with a panel portraying the bust of George Washington being crowned by neo-Classical figures of *Fame* (holding a trumpet) and *Peace* (with a palm branch), a concept taken from the practice of crowning victorious Roman generals. Then looking up you will see Brumidi's famous painting of Washington seated among Roman gods and goddesses as though he were a deified Roman emperor. It is a curious mixture of history and mythology: Mercury in his winged hat, sandals and caduceus (representing Commerce) offering a bag of money to Robert Morris to help finance the American Revolution; Neptune and Venus holding the Atlantic cable; Minerva instructing the inventor Benjamin Franklin, etc. The *Spirit of Liberty* with fasces and *Fame* or *Victory* with a trumpet stand near Washington, while thirteen maidens with stars over their heads symbolize the original States carrying a sash adorned with the motto "E pluribus unum." Nothing better illustrates the manner in which our early traditions were often portrayed in Classical, and specifically Roman, terms.

The Washington Monument
The central unit of L'Enfant's plan is a right triangle with the right angle on the Potomac and the acute angles on the President's House and Congress House. That the third point should be a commemorative equestrian statue (and not a building to house the Supreme Court, now considered the third branch of the government) indicates the importance L'Enfant attached to commemorating the inspiring figure of the Pater Patriae George Washington. This statue was never funded and after a long time it was decided to erect the obelisk that is now in approximately the same spot planned for the statue. An

The Washington Monument.
Photo: Archivio Skira.

equestrian statue was the traditional way of honoring kings and generals from Roman antiquity until the eighteenth century and in size it was consistent with Baroque notions of landscape decoration. L'Enfant perhaps had in mind a vista such as one might have had from the château at Versailles or in Paris at the Place Louis XV, where the equestrian statue of the king was much admired (by Thomas Jefferson, for one, who lived in Paris for five years). After the French Revolution, however, statues honoring monarchs fell into disfavor and that of Louis XV was pulled down and eventually replaced by a less provocative memorial, an obelisk that was sent to France (1831) as a gift from the viceroy of Egypt. This may have influenced Robert Mills when he was commissioned to design the Washington Monument a few years later. The present structure is quite different from Mills' original elaborate plan (1836), which called for a decorated Egyptian shaft 700 feet high mounted on a circular Greek temple, planned to be an American Pantheon to house statues of Presidents and national heroes. Above the east doorway there was to be a thirty-foot figure of Washington riding on a chariot like a victorious Roman general. Only six years after the laying of the cornerstone (1848), however, masked men overpowered the night-watchman and stole the marble slab from the Temple of Concord sent as a gift by Pope Pius IX. It was believed this was the work of the American party called the "Know-Nothings" angered by any involvement of the Pope in American affairs. Incidents like this, as well as the eruption of the Civil War caused work on the monument to be stopped for over twenty-five years. Thus it was not completed until 1885. Although it is much taller than ancient obelisks, it corresponds exactly in its proportions with ancient obelisks (roughly, 555 feet tall by 55 feet at the base). The Washington Monument is a true embodiment of the motto "E pluribus unum" (One from many) since many individuals and organizations throughout the United States contributed to its cost.

In the space allotted to us we cannot continue the story of how the L'Enfant's plan was adapted to the needs of a growing city and how the Mall was expanded following the centennial celebration in 1900. Throughout this period the Italian influence on the decoration of buildings has continued with rich artistry, from the nineteenth-century craftsmen and artists in the Capitol to the twentieth-century sculptors on the Washington Cathedral and mosaic experts on the National Shrine.

John Russell Pope
The Jefferson Memorial
Washington

1943

Rear of the Jefferson Memorial viewed from the park.

Completed in 1943 for the bicentennial of the birth of Thomas Jefferson, third President of the United States of America, the Memorial is located in a strategic urban position in West Potomac Park on the south shore of the Potomac River Tidal Basin.

The Memorial, together with the National Gallery of Art in Washington, is one of the final works of the American architect John Russell Pope (1874–1937) and represents both a symbol of the architectural culture that inspired Thomas Jefferson and a fundamental urban landmark within the Washington cityscape.

Standing on a massive base, the building has a circular layout surmounted by a shallow dome that shelters a bronze statue of Thomas Jefferson. It is surrounded by a portico of Ionic columns and is otherwise completely open to the elements.

The overt references to the Pantheon and to the architecture of Palladio, Jefferson's principal muse in his own architectural work, reveal the matrix that has associated this cultural and political founding father of the United States with American Classicism to the present day, establishing a linguistic and cultural thread that is clearly defined in American figurative culture.

In the overall layout of the U.S. capital, the Jefferson Memorial marks one endpoint of a fundamental axis, perpendicular to the National Mall, with the monumental and symbolic White House marking the other end.

Detail of Jefferson's statue at the center
of the Memorial.

The central position of Jefferson's statue
and the unobstructed outward views.

Overleaf
The Jefferson Memorial from the Potomac
River.

*Barbara A. Wolanin**

Italy's Presence in the United States Capitol

* *Architect of the Capitol*

Italian art and architecture, artists, and artisans, have played a major part in the beauty and symbolism of the U.S. Capitol. From the time that a new form of government and a new capital city for the United States were being conceived, the values of the Roman Republic were held as ideals. The building to house the Congress was called the Capitol, one body of the legislature was named the Senate, the stream at the bottom of the hill was renamed Tiber Creek, and Washington was thought of as a "New Rome." In 1792, President George Washington selected William Thornton's design for the new Capitol, with a center section modeled after the Pantheon in Rome. Even though the spherical contour of the dome was changed during final construction, the facade and the interior space with its oculus and coffered ceiling still recalled the temple. "The allusions to Roman architecture, landscape, and the glories of the Roman Empire created the perfect opportunity for Italian sculptors and artisans to assist in symbolizing the new nation in stone. Their imprint is strong on the Capitol, the most important American structure and the new locus of political meaning."

When carved stone column capitals, reliefs, and sculpture were designed as part of the Capitol interior by Benjamin Henry Latrobe, the new government turned to Italy, where stone carvers and sculptors were recruited to come to the United States. Giuseppe Franzoni

Room decorated by Constantino Brumidi in the Pompeian style, today used by the Senate Committee on Appropriations (S-127).
Photo: Architect of the Capitol.

John Plumbe, Jr., The United States Capitol, daguerrotype, 1846.
Library of Congress.

The *Car of History* by Carlo Franzoni
in the National Statuary Hall.
Photo: Architect of the Capitol.

Cincinnatus Called from the Plow, 1855,
by Constantino Brumidi (H-144).
Photo: Architect of the Capitol.

modeled and carved Latrobe's original corn cob and tobacco capitals, and his brother-in-law Giovanni Andrei carved Corinthian capitals. His brother Carlo Franzoni carved the graceful *Car of History*, the clock for the new Hall of the House of Representatives, and the relief of Justice for the Supreme Court Chamber. Much of the fine marble for sculpture and mantelpieces was imported, and the impressive composite capitals for the Hall of the House were carved of Carrara marble in Italy. When Charles Bulfinch completed the central building in the 1820s, the relief sculpture inside and out was carved almost entirely by Italians, including Antonio Capellano, Enrico Causici, Francesco and Luigi Persico.

A quarter of a century later, Congress decided to enlarge the Capitol by building new wings designed by Thomas U. Walter. Then in 1855, the Congress approved the construction of a new, much higher dome of cast iron, for which the dome of St. Peter's in Rome was one of Walter's inspirations. In addition to Classical architectural features used throughout, Italian marble was employed in some areas, such as one of the grand stairways, and Italian craftsmen and artists played a large role. Marble was carved and bronze cast by Italian craftsmen working on the Capitol grounds. The artist who had the greatest effect on the Capitol interior was Constantino Brumidi (1805–1880). Born in Rome, he was trained at the Academy of Saint Luke during the period of neo-Classical revival called "Purismo." He was inspired by the art of Pompeii and early Rome, Raphael, Annibale Carracci, Guido Reni, and Antonio Canova. Brumidi was considered one of the best artists in Rome, and got commissions for the Vatican and the Torlonia family. His work at the theater of the Villa Torlonia is now being restored. Caught up in the republican revolution and later imprisoned, he was pardoned by the Pope and allowed to leave the country for America in 1852. He arrived in Washington at the end of 1854 as the Capitol's new wings were being constructed and Captain Montgomery C. Meigs, the engineer in charge, was searching for an artist to paint frescoes. Brumidi's trial fresco of a Roman subject, *Cincinnatus Called from the Plow*, painted in 1855, was well received. He was put on the payroll, allowed to finish painting the entire room in true fresco, and asked to make designs for many other new rooms. He worked with teams of artists of various national origins, including the Italians Camillo Bisco, Albert Peruchi, Angelo Tonesi, and Joseph Uberti, to carry out his designs, executing all of the true frescoes himself. His murals throughout the Capitol combine Classical and allegorical subjects with portraits and scenes from American history and tributes to American values and inventions. Brumidi, who became a United States citizen in 1857, designed and executed murals for the Hall of the House of

The Brumidi Corridor on the first floor of the Senate wing inspired by Raphael's Loggia. Photo: Architect of the Capitol.

Representatives (now in H-117), the Senate Naval Affairs Committee Room (S-127), the Senate Military Affairs Committee Room (S-128), the Senate Post Office (S-211), the office of the Senate Sergeant at Arms (S-212), the Senate Reception Room (S-213), the President's Room (S-216), other office spaces, and the Senate first-floor corridors. Some blank spaces remain today because Brumidi was never allowed to complete his designs in some areas.

The second room Brumidi decorated was intended for the Senate Naval Affairs Committee (S-127), and was inspired by the first-century murals of Pompeii and of the "Baths of Titus," now known to be the Golden House of Nero, in Rome. The figures featured on the ceiling are Roman sea gods and tritons. On the walls are Pompeian maenads holding objects related to the sea, such as an anchor, pearls, or a fishing line. The maiden panels have been recently conserved, and the brilliant blue of the panels, for years painted over with dark green, is once again visible.

The vaulted, ornately decorated corridors on the first floor of the Senate wing in the United States Capitol are called the Brumidi Corridors because, although assistants and other artists are responsible for many of the details, the design of the murals and the major elements are by Constantino Brumidi. Captain Meigs directed Brumidi to carry out an elaborate decorative scheme based on Raphael's Loggia in the Vatican. The painting of the walls and ceilings of the main corridors was carried out primarily between 1857 and 1859. Within the framework of panels framed by illusionistic moldings are symmetrical designs of scrolling vines, vases, and mythological figures, inspired by Raphael's Loggia. Into these Classical motifs Brumidi integrated American flora and fauna. On the intricately decorated walls an amazing variety of Classical gods and goddesses can be seen; birds of a hundred different species; rodents, including chipmunks, squirrels, and mice; insects and reptiles; and flowers and fruits. On the ceilings are landscapes and agricultural implements interspersed among the colorful framework of ornament. Brumidi added portraits in the 1860s and frescoes over the doorways in the 1870s.

The ceiling of the President's Room (S-216) is another mural clearly inspired by Italy. In fact, Brumidi modeled the framework after the ceiling of Raphael's Stanza della Segnatura in the Vatican. The symbolic figures and cherubs seem to be siblings of Raphael's madonnas and putti. Full-length portraits of Columbus and Vespucci hold places of honor in the corners, and Benjamin Franklin reads *Poor Richard's Almanac* in Italian, a detail noted during conservation.

Brumidi worked intensively at the Capitol through the early 1860s and continued to add major frescoes through the 1870s. His most monumental contributions, the frescoed

The President's Room (S-216) has a ceiling modeled after Raphael. Photo: Architect of the Capitol.

LIBERTY.

BENJ.^{n} FRANKLIN

The office of the Speaker of the House decorated with Classical murals featuring portraits of Italian architects. Photo: Architect of the Capitol.

canopy and frieze of the new Capitol dome, were created when he was between sixty and seventy-five years old. In the canopy over the Rotunda he painted *The Apotheosis of George Washington* in 1865. The fresco depicts the first President rising to the heavens, flanked by Liberty/Authority and Victory/Fame, with their traditional symbols. On the earth below, Roman gods and goddesses interact with figures from American history and new technology. Minerva counsels Benjamin Franklin, Samuel F. B. Morse, and Robert Fulton as an electric generator is demonstrated. Neptune and Venus help to lay the Atlantic Cable to carry telegraph signals across the Ocean. Venus is clearly reminiscent of Raphael's Galatea in the Farnesina Palace.

Brumidi began painting the frieze depicting major events in American history in 1878 but died in 1880 with the work less than half finished. His remaining designs were carried out between 1881 and 1889 by Filippo Costaggini, another Roman painter trained at the Academy of Saint Luke. Brumidi designed the frieze to look like a sculptured relief, painted in dark browns and whites, perhaps inspired by the Column of Trajan.

In 1897, almost twenty years after Brumidi's death, the Library of Congress was moved out of the Capitol and into its own building, now called the Thomas Jefferson Building. Constructed in Renaissance style, it is filled with Classical architectural details and murals, mostly painted in oil on canvas, by leading American artists. Many Italian craftsmen worked carving marble cherubs and laying the mosaic floors.

In the early 1900s, after the Library moved out, the West Central Front of the Capitol was reconstructed and other areas were redecorated. The West Central Front contains murals with Classical motifs, including garlands, rinceaux, and cherubs, designed by Elmer Garnsey. The fireplaces were outfitted with marble mantelpieces and mantel mirrors with classical columns and friezes. Other areas in the Capitol were decorated in this period by one of Brumidi's early assistants, Joseph Rakemann.

In 1985, the Architect of the Capitol began a program to systematically clean Brumidi's murals of grime, discolored coatings, and heavy-handed overpainting, revealing their original beauty and high quality and allowing the appreciation of his genius. The Italian artist's 200th birthday was celebrated by the Congress with a ceremony in the Rotunda, beneath his frescoes, which are among the murals, sculptures, and architectural elements in the U.S. Capitol that owe so much to the legacy of Italy.

Sources

William C. Allen, *History of the United States Capitol: A Chronicle of Design, Construction, and Politics* (Washington: Government Printing Office, 2001).

Alberta Campitelli, *Villa Torlonia* (Rome: Istituto Poligrafico e Zecca dello Stato, Libreria dello Stato, 1997).

William Dickinson, Dean A. Herrin, and Donald R. Kennon, eds., *Montgomery C. Meigs and the Building of the Nation's Capital* (Athens: Ohio University Press for the United States Capitol Historical Society, 2001).

Viven Green Fryd, *Art and Empire: The Politics of Ethnicity in the U.S. Capitol, 1815–1860* (New Haven: Yale University Press, 1992).

Donald R. Kennon and Thomas P. Somma, eds., *American Pantheon: Sculptural and Artistic Decoration of the United States Capitol* (Athens: Ohio University Press for the United States Capitol Historical Society, 2004).

Donald R. Kennon, ed., *The United States Capitol: Designing and Decorating a National Icon* (Athens: Ohio University Press for the United States Capitol His-

torical Society, 2000).

Myrtle Murdock, *Constantino Brumidi, Michelangelo of the United States Capitol* (Washington: Monumental Press, 1950).

Henry Hope Reed, *The United States Capitol: Its Architecture and Decoration* (New York: W. W. Norton & Company, 2005).

Pamela Scott, *Temple of Liberty: Building the Capitol for a New Nation* (New York: Oxford University Press, 1995).

Barbara Wolanin, *Constantino Brumidi: Artist of the Capitol* (Washington: Government Printing Office, 1998).

The Frescoes by Constantino Brumidi in the U.S. Capitol

1855–1880

Decorations in the inner dome and canopy over the Rotunda.
Photo: Architect of the Capitol.

Overleaf
The Apotheosis of George Washington painted under the dome and detail showing the scene of Commerce with the Roman god Mercury.

The frescoed frieze. Crowd listening to the reading of the Declaration of Independence (*left*); the figures of America and History (*below*).

David Alan Brown
and Maygene Daniels*

Italia and America at the National Gallery of Art

* Curator of Italian Paintings
and Chief of Gallery Archives

From its inception, the National Gallery of Art has been inspired and influenced by the Italian tradition in art and architecture. The Gallery was founded by financier, public servant, and art collector Andrew W. Mellon (1855–1937), who in December 1936 offered to build a national art museum in Washington with his own funds and to donate his superb collection as the nucleus of its holdings. At that time, nearly half of the works of painting and sculpture in Mellon's collection were by Italian artists.

Mellon envisioned a museum that would blend private generosity with public ownership and support. He stipulated that the new institution should not bear his name but should be called the National Gallery of Art to encourage gifts from other donors and to ensure that it would continue to grow. Early in 1937 President Franklin D. Roosevelt recommended that Mellon's gift be accepted and in March of that year the new National Gallery of Art was established by the United States Congress.

Mellon selected American architect John Russell Pope (1874–1937) to design the Gallery's West Building. The style of Pope's public buildings was deeply influenced by classical Italian architecture. As a young architecture student, he spent two years at the American Academy in Rome where he studied many of the most important buildings of Italy. Following these influential years, he refined his skills of formal planning and classical composition during two additional years of study at the École des Beaux-Art in Paris, graduating in 1900.

Pope was an eclectic designer, able to work in a range of historical styles as the occasion required. Yet, like others of his generation, he was convinced that classical architecture such as that of ancient Rome was the best possible expression of the American ideals of democracy and humanism, and his monumental buildings in Washington and elsewhere were nearly always indebted to classical precedents.

When Mellon selected Pope to design the building for the new Gallery, the architect had recently completed the nearby National Archives building, whose elaborate Corinthian columns and porticoes lent dignity to Constitution Avenue. Pope's Jefferson Memorial near the Potomac River, directly south of the White House, was begun three years before the Gallery but was not finished until 1943, two years after the museum had opened. In his design for the memorial Pope employed a classical temple portico and a shallow dome, forms also used for the West Building.

In late 1935 and 1936 Pope quickly established the essential elements of his design for the Gallery, conceiving the building in a style of spare, refined classicism reflecting his admiration for Roman prototypes. His plan envisioned a symmetrical design centered on a dome with columned porticoes on all four sides of the building. Although the end porticoes were later dropped from the design at Andrew Mellon's request, those on the building's north and south facades remained as prominent exterior features.

The architect gave equal consideration to the layout of the building's interior, centering it on a domed Rotunda. His plan called for a pair of high, skylit sculpture halls to

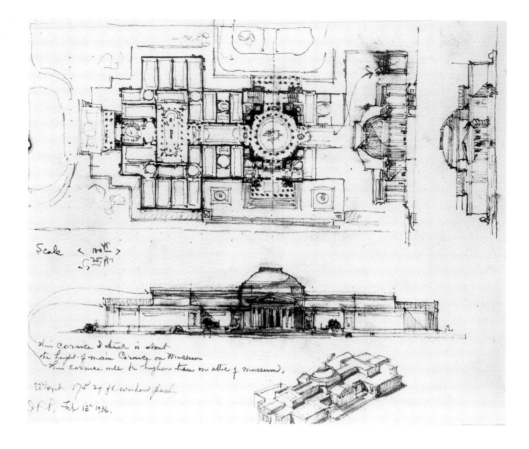

extend east and west from the Rotunda, forming the main circulation spine for the building. These in turn were to open into a network of smaller exhibition rooms. Skylit garden courts at each end of the building would offer restful havens for visitors.

The direct influence of Italian precedents can be found throughout Pope's design. The central Rotunda, the most important space in the structure, is modeled after the ancient Pantheon in Rome, echoing its balanced proportions and coffered plaster dome and oculus. Other details in the Rotunda suggest Italian sources. Twenty-four dramatic Ionic columns support a formal entablature with the dome above. Pilasters, moldings, and niches inspired by classical examples articulate the interior walls.

In keeping with the beaux-arts tradition in which Pope had been trained, the architects paid careful attention to the building's interior materials. Italian stone is prominent throughout. The Rotunda's columns are of dark green Verte Imperial marble quarried near Lucca. The blocks of marble were skidded down the mountainside and transferred on railway cars to Italian docks where they were shipped to the United States just before the outbreak of the Second World War disrupted ocean transport. The column drums were cut and turned in Vermont before finally being assembled on-site in Washington. Buff-colored Italian Botticino marble was used for the columns' strongly contrasting Ionic capitals and bases. Other carefully selected Italian marbles were employed in stairs and lobbies.

Andrew Mellon had wanted visitors to the Gallery to enjoy and learn from its art collections, and he believed this would be encouraged by displaying paintings in rooms that were finished in styles appropriate to the nation and era in which the works had been created. In keeping with this idea, twenty-seven rooms were designed specifically for the display of Italian paintings and sculptures. Italian travertine, in all approximately 25,000 cubic feet, was used for their wainscoting and trim.

The designers gave special attention to creating a suitable exhibition room for Raphael's *Alba Madonna*, which Andrew Mellon had purchased from the Hermitage

Michelangelo's *David / Apollo* in its crate arriving for exhibition at the National Gallery of Art, December 1948.
Courtesy of the National Gallery of Art, Washington.

Museum in 1931. Initially the architect proposed that the painting should hang in a niche, with pilasters on either side and a patterned brocade on the walls. Eventually, a simpler and more flexible arrangement was approved with travertine wainscoting and unadorned plaster surfaces similar to the other rooms for Italian works.

Neither Andrew Mellon nor John Russell Pope lived to see the new building completed. Both died in August 1937, more than three years before the museum opened to the public, yet both would have been pleased had they been able to see it. When it opened, the building was celebrated for its "noble grandeur" and quickly became one of the most popular destinations for visitors to Washington. Within the museum, Samuel H. Kress' great collection of Italian Renaissance art, including 375 paintings and 18 works of sculpture, had joined Andrew Mellon's art in the exhibition rooms. Thus when President Franklin D. Roosevelt accepted the museum and its collections on behalf of the nation on March 17, 1941, a spectacular assemblage of Italian painting and sculpture already was on view.

The Gallery had opened on the eve of American entry into World War II. Less than ten months later, in January 1942, its most important works, including many by Italian artists, were moved for safekeeping to Biltmore House in Asheville, North Carolina. Yet except for the small group of evacuated works, the museum's collection, including more than three hundred Italian paintings and sculptures, remained on view throughout the conflict as the Gallery opened its doors to thousands of young men and women in the armed forces. Echoing the thoughts of many, one serviceman wrote of his visit: "No war here, for art outlives war."

In 1948, as normalcy returned to Europe, Italian leaders began to look for ways to express their nation's gratitude to the United States for postwar assistance. Recognizing the symbolic importance of the nation's great artistic tradition, they decided that the most appropriate gesture would be to loan one of Italy's most famous art treasures to the Gallery, where it could be viewed and appreciated by the leaders and citizens of the United States close to home. In keeping with this decision, by mid-1948, Italian officials were making detailed plans to transport Michelangelo's *David/Apollo* from the Museo del Bargello in Florence to the Gallery to reaffirm the friendship and cultural ties between the peoples of Italy and the United States. As 1948 drew to a close, the statue was carefully packed in Florence and carried by rail to Naples. The United States Navy transported the sculpture to Norfolk on the USS *Grand Canyon*. Finally it was escorted by military convoy on the ultimate leg of its trip, arriving at the Gallery early in the morning of December 24, 1948. The convoy was filmed by Movietone News.

At the Gallery, Michelangelo's sculpture was welcomed by an honor guard of United States Marines joined by representatives of the Italian Embassy and officers of the Gallery. It was installed on a specially designed pedestal adjacent to the West Garden Court. When President Harry S. Truman held his inaugural reception at the museum on January 20, 1949, more than 8,000 guests viewed the magnificent work of art. In all it was seen by more than three-quarters of a million visitors during its stay in Washington before being returned to Florence in late June. The loan remains today a lasting symbol of the ongoing friendship between the two nations.

Since the dramatic visit of Michelangelo's famous sculpture, the Gallery has continued to present the art of Italy to the people of the United States in special exhibitions and through its own collection. In size, scope, and quality, the Gallery's collection of Italian paintings is regarded as the most important in America, and it counts among the finest and most comprehensive collections of its kind in the world. But the Italian paintings were not acquired, as might be expected, one by one during the decades after the Gallery was founded in 1937. Instead, the holdings in this area result mainly from the confluence of three great collections formed in the first half of the twentieth century. Andrew Mellon's original bequest of 1937 included some 36 Italian paintings, while Joseph Widener's donation five years later added 25 further examples. Most of the Gallery's Italian art, however, was donated by Samuel H. Kress and the foundation named after him. Many of these works came to America from British private collections via the dealer Sir Joseph Duveen. Another source was the Florentine Count Alessandro Contini Bonacossi, who supplied pictures to Kress. Since the Italian masters had always been highly prized, the Americans faced the problem of how, coming so late, they might still acquire Italian art of the finest quality. Fortunately, exceptional opportunities arose when authorities de-accessioned some of the greatest treasures belonging to three European museums. In 1931 an international consortium of dealers acting on behalf of Andrew Mellon purchased Botticelli's *Adoration of the Magi*, Perugino's *Crucifixion with Saints*, Titian's *Venus with a Mirror*, and Raphael's *St. George and the Dragon* and the *Alba Madonna*, a harmoniously balanced masterpiece from his Roman period, together with sixteen other outstanding works, from the Hermitage Museum, Leningrad (now St. Petersburg). Likewise in the late 1930s, the Kaiser Friedrich Museum in Berlin sold Duccio's *Nativity with the Prophets Isaiah and Ezekiel* and Filippo Lippi's *Madonna and Child* to Duveen, who in turn sold them to Mellon and Kress respectively. In the same manner, Kress obtained Raphael's striking portrait of *Bindo Altoviti* from the Alte Pinakothek in Munich. Acquisitions of this caliber went far toward raising America's new Gallery to the level of the great European museums it hoped to rival.

Duveen employed the foremost authority on Italian paintings, Bernard Berenson (1865–1959), to authenticate the acquisitions of his millionaire clients. An exhibition held at the Gallery in 1979 explored Berenson's role in forming American taste and collections through his influential writings and expertise. J. Carter Brown, the Gallery's director from 1969 to 1992, observed that this institution was "more directly a product of [Berenson's] eye and taste than many realize, for during its period of rapid acquisition in the Italian field he was virtually an adjunct curator." Indeed, Brown's predecessor, John Walker, had been a disciple at Berenson's Villa I Tatti outside Florence and later, as director, often turned to his mentor for advice.

Berenson's role in enhancing the prestige of the Italian masters on this side of the Atlantic may also be seen in the fact that Andrew Mellon, despite a partiality for Dutch landscapes and English portraits, nevertheless acquired major Italian pictures. Inspired by the National Gallery, London, Mellon understood that to be representative, the new gallery he envisaged for Washington had to present Italian painting. Berenson played a more direct role in forming the Old Master collection assembled by Joseph Widener and his father. The elder Widener, who had made a fortune in urban mass transit, began to purchase pictures in the 1890s. With Berenson's advice father and son disposed of less significant examples and brought together a choice group of Italian paintings, which were displayed in a setting of Renaissance furniture and decorative arts at their estate outside Philadelphia.

If the Wideners, like Mellon, favored the Grand Manner, the last of the Gallery's three major Old Master painting collectors, Samuel H. Kress seems to have particularly admired Italian paintings, acquiring them systematically. Indeed, he aimed to form the largest and most comprehensive series of these works in private hands. Kress, a dime-store magnate, originally intended to form a private museum but was persuaded instead to join his holdings to those of Mellon in the newly established Gallery. Ranging from the fifteenth through the eighteenth centuries, the Kress pictures greatly outnumber those brought together by Mellon and Widener. By 1941, when the Gallery opened to the public, his collection consisted of some 375 Italian paintings. In 1943, Kress explained that he hoped to

"be able to continue my efforts in helping to build up the Gallery Collection at least in the Italian School, since, as you know, it is the principal school in European collections and is therefore shown most prominently at those museums." Kress' decision to bring his collection to Washington led to an extensive revision of his holdings over a period of years, with the more important examples generally retained for the Gallery and the others dispersed to museums elsewhere in the country. Despite the exceptionally broad range of the Kress Collection, its primary focus remained Italian painting. Samuel Kress' lifelong devotion to early Italian art may be seen not only in the sheer number of such works he brought together but also in the manner in which it was displayed in a neo-Renaissance interior in his New York apartment—a fitting setting for a merchant prince on the model of the Medici.

Following the period of growth by large increments, the Gallery's acquisitions of early Italian paintings have been few. A notable exception was in 1967, when with funds provided by Ailsa Mellon Bruce, the Gallery purchased Leonardo da Vinci's double-sided *Ginevra de' Benci* from the princely Liechtenstein Collection, and the only Leonardo painting in the Western Hemisphere instantly became the Gallery's most famous picture. While this sensational purchase continued the bias toward earlier Italian painting reflected in the Mellon and Widener Collections, the Kress Collection, particularly in the way it was extended by Samuel's brother Rush and by the Kress Foundation, includes many fine Italian paintings of the seventeenth and eighteenth centuries. Orazio Gentileschi's *Lute Player*, for example, has been called his masterpiece. It is in this area of Italian

A page from Giorgio Vasari's *Libro de' Disegni*, with drawings by Botticelli, Filippino Lippi, and Raffaellino del Garbo, late fifteenth century (drawings) and mid-sixteenth century (mount). Woodner Collection, Patrons' Permanent Fund. Courtesy of the National Gallery of Art, Washington.

Baroque painting that the Gallery has most assiduously collected in the last three decades. Bernardo Bellotto's *The Fortress of Koenigstein*, Corrado Giaquinto's allegories of *Autumn* and *Winter*, and Guercino's newly discovered *Self-portrait*, among others, are helping to fill the gap in this previously neglected field.

Although shorn of the furniture and decorative arts that once surrounded them, the Italian paintings are shown today in the remarkably harmonious environment provided by John Russell Pope's serenely classicizing West Building. The pictures are arranged chronologically following the standard art-historical designations of medieval, Renaissance, and Baroque. Thus a visit to the Gallery ideally begins with such masterpieces as Giotto's *Madonna* or the already-mentioned *Nativity* from Duccio's celebrated *Maestà* polyptych carried in triumph to Siena Cathedral in 1311. Highlights from the early Renaissance include the tondo of the *Adoration of the Magi*, combining the talents of Fra Angelico and Filippo Lippi, in all likelihood the most highly valued picture in Lorenzo de' Medici's collection.

Outside Florence, other centers developed their own versions of the Renaissance. In Venice Giovanni Bellini painted the Gallery's famous *Feast of the Gods* as the first of a series of mythologies for the Duke of Ferrara's private study. Technical investigation of this canvas reveals that the landscape was overpainted by Titian. The variety of regional styles in North Italy—Tura, Dosso, Moretto, and Moroni—is very well displayed at the Gallery, while Central Italian painting is headed by no fewer than five works by Raphael, the largest group in America. Also represented by numerous fine examples are Titian, Bernardino Luini, and, from a later period, Tiepolo and Canaletto.

Along with its splendid Italian paintings, the National Gallery of Art has extensive holdings of Italian sculpture, free-standing or in relief and in marble, bronze, and other materials. Again, the emphasis is on the Italian Renaissance, and the principal donors—Mellon, Widener, and Kress—are the same ones who provided the Italian paintings. Headed by Leon Battista Alberti's celebrated bronze *Self-portrait* relief, the Florentine School is especially well represented with examples by Desiderio da Settignano, Mino da Fiesole, Antonio Rossellino, and Verrocchio. A large number of these works came from the famous collection put together by Gustave Dreyfus early in the last century. That collection was also the source for the majority of the Gallery's portrait medals, including an outstanding group by Pisanello. If, like the paintings, the Gallery's Italian sculpture boasts a strength in Florence, artists like Francesco di Giorgio from Siena and Riccio from Padua are also present. The Italian sculpture culminates in Bernini's dazzling marble portrait bust of Monsignor Francesco Barberini. Displayed together with the sculpture in the Gallery's newly renovated ground-floor sculpture galleries is a fine selection of the decorative earthenware known as maiolica.

For many years after its founding, the National Gallery of Art did not actively collect drawings, but in recent decades a concerted effort has been made to bring the graphics collection up to the level of the paintings. Stellar examples in the Italian field are Cellini's extraordinary *Satyr* and the page from Vasari's *Libro de' Disegni*, with figure studies by Botticelli and Filippino Lippi, both in the Woodner Collection. The Gallery can also now boast the finest collection of Mantegna's engravings outside Europe.

In less than three-quarters of a century the National Gallery of Art has become a great museum with superb collections of Italian art. Through the years, the museum has complemented its own growing collections with a series of international loan exhibitions, which have brought the art of Italy from abroad to be showcased in Washington. Housed in a museum building inspired by the precedents of ancient Rome, the National Gallery of Art stands as a reminder of the enduring influence of Italian art and architecture on the United States and its culture.

Loan Exhibitions of Italian Art at the National Gallery of Art

Since 1942 Italian art has figured prominently in the National Gallery of Art's far-ranging exhibition program. The Gallery has brought to the United States some of Italy's most celebrated masterpieces, such as Leonardo da Vinci's *Mona Lisa* (1503–06) and *Portrait of a Lady with an Ermine (Cecilia Gallerani)* (c. 1490) and Michelangelo's *David/Apollo* (c. 1530), while also presenting important surveys of works by Bellini, Bernini, Desiderio, Giorgione, Guercino, Leonardo, Lotto, Michelangelo, Raphael, Titian, and Veronese, among others.

1945
Italian Eighteenth-Century Prints, February 28–May 21, 1945

1949
Michelangelo's David, from the Bargello Museum, Florence, January 24–June 28, 1949
Early Italian Engravings, April 17–June 19, 1949

1957
Illuminated Manuscript Pages and North Italian Engravings, December 21, 1957–February 1, 1958

1960
Italian Drawings: Masterpieces from Five Centuries, October 9–November 6, 1960
Italian Prints, October 9–November 6, 1960

1961
Etchings and Drawings by Giovanni Battista Tiepolo and Giovanni Domenico Tiepolo, September 15–November 2, 1961

Tiepolo Drawings, September 17–October 15, 1961

1962
Etchings by G. B. Tiepolo, G. D. Tiepolo, and Canaletto, October 27, 1962–June 11, 1963

1963
Mona Lisa by Leonardo da Vinci, January 8–February 3, 1963
Hercules and the Hydra and Hercules and Antaeus by Antonio del Pollaiuolo, February 4–February 10, 1963
Eighteenth-Century Venetian Drawings from the Correr Museum, October 27–November 24, 1963
Eighteenth-Century Venetian Etchings from the National Gallery of Art Collection, October 27–November 24, 1963

1964
Piranesi Etchings of Prisons and Views of Rome from the National Gallery of Art Collection, November 4, 1964–April 18, 1965

1966
Piranesi Etchings from the Collection of the National Gallery of Art, August 13, 1966–March 30, 1967
Canaletto and Bellotto Etchings from the Collection of the National Gallery of Art, October 12, 1966–April 24, 1967

1971
G. B. Piranesi: Etchings of Prisons, Views of Rome from the National Gallery of Art Collection, May 5–July 28, 1971
La Scala: 400 Years of Stage Design from the Museo Teatrale alla Scala, Milan, September 11–October 17, 1971

1972

Rare Etchings by G. B. and G. D. Tiepolo,
January 25–April 23, 1972

1973

Prints of the Italian Renaissance, June
24–October 7, 1973
*Venetian Views: Etchings by Canaletto and
Whistler,* July 12–December 26, 1973
*Sixteenth-Century Italian Drawings from the
Collection of Janos Scholz,* September
23–November 25, 1973

1974

Art in the Age of Francesco Petrarca, April
6–13, 1974
*Venetian Drawings from American
Collections,* September 29–November 24,
1974

1976

Titian and the Venetian Woodcut, October 30,
1976–January 2, 1977

1978

Piranesi: The Early Architectural Fantasies,
June 1–September 30, 1978

1979

*Berenson and the Connoisseurship of Italian
Painting,* January 21–September 3, 1979
*Prints and Related Drawings by the Carracci
Family,* March 18–May 20, 1979
*From Leonardo to Titian: Italian Renaissance
Paintings from the Hermitage, Leningrad,* May
13–June 24, 1979
*Italian Drawings in the Art Institute of
Chicago,* December 9, 1979–March 2, 1980

1980

Italian Drawings 1780–1890, March 16–May
11, 1980

1981

The Drawings of Andrea Palladio, May
17–July 5, 1981

1982

*Sixteenth-Century Italian Maiolica from the
Arthur M. Sackler Collection and the National
Gallery of Art's Widener Collection,*
September 5, 1982–January 9, 1983

1983

Raphael and America, January 9–May 8, 1983
*Painting in Naples from Caravaggio to
Giordano,* February 13–May 1, 1983
Piazzetta: A Tercentenary Exhibition of

Drawings, Prints, and Illustrated Books,
November 20, 1983–March 4, 1984
Modigliani: An Anniversary Exhibition,
December 11, 1983–April 22, 1984
Leonardo's Last Supper: Before and After,
December 18, 1983–March 4, 1984

1984

Caravaggio's Deposition from the Vatican,
March 4–April 29, 1984
*The Legacy of Correggio: Sixteenth-Century
Emilian Drawings,*
March 11–May 13, 1984
*Renaissance Drawings from the Ambrosiana,
1370–1600,* August 12–October 7, 1984

1985

*Leonardo da Vinci Drawings of Horses from
the Royal Library at Windsor Castle,* February
24–June 9, 1985

1986

Titian: The Flaying of Marsyas, January
17–April 20, 1986
*The Age of Correggio and the Carracci:
Emilian Painting of the Sixteenth and
Seventeenth Centuries,* December 19,
1986–February 16, 1987

1987

Donatello at Close Range, April 3–June 15,
1987
*Italian Master Drawings from the British
Royal Collection,* May 10–July 26, 1987
*Rosso Fiorentino: Drawings, Prints, and
Decorative Arts,* October 25, 1987–January 3,
1988
Titian's Saint Sebastian, December 6,
1987–February 17, 1988

1988

Michelangelo: Draftsman/Architect, October
9–December 11, 1988
*The Pastoral Landscape: The Legacy of
Venice,* November 6, 1988–January 22, 1989
The Art of Paolo Veronese, 1528–1588,
November 13, 1988–February 20, 1989

1989

*Italian Etchers of the Renaissance and
Baroque: Parmigianino to Giordano,*
September 24–November
26, 1989

1990

*Reinstallation of Bellini/Titian Feast of the
Gods,* January 14–May 13, 1990 (extended
from April 29)

Selected Baroque Paintings from Italian Banks, September 26–November 26, 1990 (extended from November 11)
Titian, Prince of Painters, October 28, 1990–January 27, 1991

1991
Circa 1492: Art in the Age of Exploration, October 12, 1991–January 12, 1992
Italian Drawings from the Armand Hammer Collection, November 17, 1991–May 10, 1992

1992
Guercino: Drawings from Windsor Castle, March 15–May 17, 1992
Guercino: Master Painter of the Baroque, March 15–May 17, 1992

1993
Giambologna's Cesarini Venus, September 26, 1993–May 15, 1994
Italian Drawings from the Armand Hammer Collection, November 14, 1993–May 8, 1994

1994
Italian Renaissance Architecture: Brunelleschi, Sangallo, Michelangelo—The Cathedrals of Florence and Pavia and Saint Peter's, Rome, December 18, 1994–April 16, 1995

1995
The Glory of Venice: Art in the Eighteenth Century, January 29–April 23, 1995
Italian Drawings from the Armand Hammer Collection, November 19, 1995–May 5, 1996

1996
Masterpieces from the Palazzo Doria Pamphilj, Rome, June 16–September 2, 1996
Michelangelo and His Influence: Drawings from Windsor Castle, October 27, 1996–January 5, 1997

1997
Lorenzo Lotto: Rediscovered Master of the Renaissance, November 2, 1997–March 1, 1998

1998
Bernini's Rome: Italian Baroque Terracottas from the State Hermitage Museum, St. Petersburg, October 11, 1998–January 18, 1999

1999
Caravaggio's The Taking of Christ: Saints and Sinners in Baroque Painting, May 30–July 18, 1999

The Drawings of Annibale Carracci, September 26, 1999–January 9, 2000

2000
Raphael and His Circle: Drawings from Windsor Castle, May 14–July 23, 2000
Italian Drawings from the Armand Hammer Collection, November 16, 2000–May 13, 2001

2001
Virtue and Beauty: Leonardo's "Ginevra de Benci" and Renaissance Portraits of Women, September 30, 2001–January 6, 2002

2002
The Flowering of Florence: Botanical Art for the Medici, March 3–May 27, 2002
Renaissance Bronzes from the Robert H. Smith Collection, September 29, 2002–February 17, 2003
Italian Drawings from the Armand Hammer Collection, November 10, 2002–May 5, 2003

2004
Verrocchio's David Restored: A Renaissance Bronze from the National Museum of the Bargello, Florence, February 13–March 21, 2004
Italian Drawings from the Armand Hammer Collection, November 21, 2004–May 8, 2005

2005
Monumental Sculpture from Renaissance Florence: Ghiberti, Nanni di Banco, and Verrocchio at Orsanmichele, September 18, 2005–February 26, 2006 (extended from December 31, 2005)

2006
The Poetry of Light: Venetian Drawings from the National Gallery of Art, April 30–October 1, 2006
Bellini, Giorgione, Titian, and the Renaissance of Venetian Painting, June 18–September 17, 2006

2007
Desiderio da Settignano, July 1–October 8, 2007

museum of modern art bulletin   *Olivetti: design in industry*

Paolo Scrivano*

Romanticizing the Other?
Views of Italian Industrial Design in Postwar America

* Professor, Boston University,
Art History Department

In a 1938 article for the revue *Verve*, the French poet and writer Paul Valéry defined the notion of "Orient" as typified by the "quality of pure wonder". "If this name is to have its full and entire effect on the mind—he wrote—one must ... *never have been* in the ill-designed region it designates."[1] In Valéry's view, "Orient" was a concept unassociated to any specific geographical reality. This most inexplicable entity, he specified, "must be known only from pictures, from stories one has heard or read, and from a few objects; and then only in the least erudite, most inexact, and even muddled fashion."[2] The term "Orient" may appear inappropriate to describe the case of Italy, although recently it has been used to refer to the unequal social and economic dynamics between the northern and southern parts of the peninsula.[3] But if we go to the spirit of Valéry's definition, which tacitly acknowledges that trans-cultural connections are conditioned by only partial understandings, it is not farfetched to assume that the perception of Italy from abroad is indicative of a sort of "orientalism." There is no doubt that the representation of Italian culture on the part of foreigners has been regularly characterized by images that reflect more often than not the observer's predisposition than the reality under observation. This fraught tendency to "romanticize the other" might well be illustrated by how America has seen Italy in the past and still sees it today.

The way Italian industrial design was received in the United States in the postwar years serves as an apt example. While in the decade following the end of the Second World War Italy became one of the major recipients of Marshall Plan's funds (with almost 11% of the resources allocated worldwide), American ideas about Italian architectural and design culture remained by and large anchored in a highly nostalgic pre-industrial view, regardless of the condition in which the country actually lay at the end of the conflict and during the years of the reconstruction. The exhibition *Italy at Work: Her Renaissance in Design Today*, one of the first events to present Italian "industrial" design to American audiences, is a good case in point. Opening at the Art Institute of Chicago from March to May 1951 and circulating afterwards in various cities including Baltimore, Houston, and New York, the show depicted Italian manufacturing mainly as producing high-quality handicrafts.[4] In a display dominated by inlaid decorations, ceramics, jewels, and embroideries by the likes of artists and artisans such as Pietro Cascella, Enrico Bernardi, and Alfredo Barbini, the representation of design associated with mass-production was limited to a Lambretta scooter and some Olivetti typewriters. It is not surprising that projects by Gio Ponti or Carlo Mollino, authors whose work leaned more towards the realization of *unica* than towards the investigation of the evolving connection between design and mass-manufacturing and mass-consumption, were called upon to represent "official" architectural culture.[5]

In selecting the material for display and in preparing the exhibition, the curators of *Italy at Work* had assumed an interpretation of Italian design culture (if not of Italian culture *tout court*) tainted by simplifications and generalizations: modern production was grounded on—in the organizers' words— "ancient traditions" and postwar goods were the

Olivetti: Design in Industry, issue no. 20
of *The Museum of Modern Art Bulletin*, 1952.
Volume design by Leo Lionni in collaboration
with the Department of Architecture and
Design of the Museum of Modern Art.

157

Meyric R. Rogers, *Italy at Work: Her Renaissance in Design Today*, exhibition catalogue, Art Institute of Chicago, 1950. Cover design by Corrado Cagli.

George E. Kidder Smith, *Italy Builds: Its Modern Architecture and Native Inheritance*, 1955. Cover design by Leo Lionni.

result of "the deep cultural soil in which the Italian arts are rooted."[6] The motivations for organizing the show were evinced in the opening paragraph of the catalogue accompanying the event: "The Italian is an individualist. Hence this exhibition."[7] It was not uncommon during the 1950s to encounter these kinds of stereotypical assumptions in publications dedicated to architecture. An interesting example in this regard is provided by the well-known book *Italy Builds*, authored by the American photographer and critic George Everard Kidder Smith and published in 1954 in both Italian and English languages.[8] The book was thought to provide English-speaking audiences with an empirical report on the state of Italy's postwar architecture: in describing local production, the author remarked upon the "intellectual depth" of the most prominent architects, the "integration with painting and sculpture," the "felicitous mixture of new and old," and the "freedom from clichés and dogmas." Kidder Smith offered a rather precise portrait of Italian architecture, one that read less emotional and passionate than the preface to the book written by Ernesto Nathan Rogers.[9] This enthusiastic endorsement of Italian postwar architecture, however, did not prevent the author from falling into the trap of romanticizing and stereotyping the object of his attentions. In a revealing passage of *Italy Builds*, for example, Kidder Smith tried to attenuate his criticism of Italian architecture for its supposed "lack of consideration for occupants" in a way that conversely unveiled his partially concealed prejudices: "If privacy, peace and quiet mean little to anyone—he wrote—who cares if the bedrooms are plastered along noisy streets and sidewalks?"[10] Predictably, these views were seldom received with eagerness in Italy: in reviewing Kidder Smith's volume, a young Francesco Tentori deemed the Italian version of *Italy Builds* simply as "useless."[11]

If there was an image of Italian design emerging in the United States during the postwar years, this was not only due to American-led initiatives. By mounting commercial

Marcello Nizzoli and Giuseppe Beccio,
Olivetti Lexicon 80 typewriter, 1948.
Archivio Storico Olivetti, Ivrea.

Marcello Nizzoli and Giuseppe Beccio,
Olivetti Lettera 22 typewriter, 1950.
Archivio Storico Olivetti, Ivrea.

BBPR, Olivetti showroom, New York, 1954.
Archivio Storico Olivetti, Ivrea.

BBPR, Olivetti showroom, New York, 1954, In
the background Costantino Nivola's bas-relief.
Archivio Storico Olivetti, Ivrea.

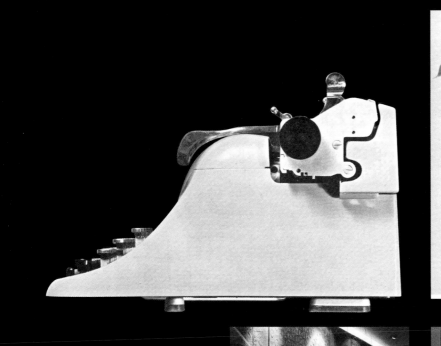

Gio Ponti, Alitalia premises, New York, 1958.
Ceramics and terracottas by Fausto Melotti
and Salvatore Fiume. From Lisa Licitra Ponti,
Gio Ponti: The Complete Work 1923–1978
(Cambridge, Mass.: The MIT Press, 1990),
p. 178.

Italy: The New Domestic Landscape,
exhibition catalogue, Museum of Modern Art,
New York, 1972. Volume design by
Emilio Ambasz and Centro Di.

campaigns aimed at penetrating transatlantic markets, the Olivetti company played a significant role in familiarizing the U.S. public to industrial design of Italian origin. While Olivetti's production had arguably gained some visibility among North-American users and designers in the prewar and early postwar years, it was the exhibition organized in 1952 by the Museum of Modern Art in New York that made popular the name of the Italian manufacturer. With an installation designed by Leo Lionni, the show not only displayed famous artifacts such as the Lexicon 80 typewriter, but gave the Museum the opportunity to portray the Olivetti company as "the leading corporation in the western world in the field of design."[12] Together with this exhibition, Olivetti's strategy of opening retail shops in major American cities helped boost the status of Italian design within the United States. The showroom in New York, inaugurated in 1954 on Fifth Avenue between 47th and 48th Streets, became a trademark of the Italian company in North America, even if at the time writer and critic Lewis Mumford criticized the project by the Milanese firm BBPR for lacking "human touch."[13] Still, Olivetti's reputation was rooted in an "exotic" perception of Italian design culture, one that seemed to evoke the "otherness" of its aesthetic and formal attitudes. Significantly, the successor of the Olivetti showroom in New York, Gio Ponti's Alitalia office of 1958 (a few blocks away from the former), allegedly recreated a "particularly Italian" internal environment by the use of custom-made terracottas and ceramics.[14]

The discrepancy between reality and imagination in the way Italian design culture was presented to the American public is made evident by the societal and economic transformations Italy underwent during these years. Under pressure to increase demands for consumer goods, industries such as those manufacturing domestic electric-appliances became key segments for the national economy. For example, Italian production of refrigerators went from 18,500 units in 1951 to 370,000 in 1957, and 3,200,000 in 1967.[15] The combination of factors like the availability of cheap labor with relatively high technical skills and the low level of financial investment implied in the domestic appliances' production granted success to a sector whose contribution to the field of industrial design has often been underrated, despite its important commercial achievements.[16] Although between the end of the 1960s and the beginning of the 1970s Italian designers and design

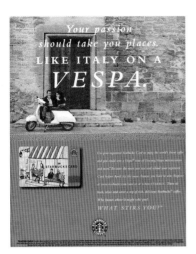

Advertisement for Starbucks from *The New York Times Magazine* (April 13, 2003), p. 23.

Advertisement for luxury residences in Bal Harbour, Florida, from *The New York Times Magazine* (January 19, 2003), p. 65.

Advertisement for luxury residences in Bal Harbour, Florida, from *The New York Times Magazine* (January 26, 2003), p. 63.

theorists began to address the questions prompted by the advance of consumer society, the images that circulated in the United States remained attached to a typecasting that had endured since the 1940s and 1950s. When at a distance of two decades from the show dedicated to Olivetti, another exhibition held at the Museum of Modern Art—*Italy: The New Domestic Landscape*, curated by Emilio Ambasz[17]—tried to break away from the persistent anachronisms representing Italian design culture by embracing a fresh critical stance, it merely reinforced pre-existing perceptions: "radical" approaches such as those of Alessandro Mendini or Superstudio simply accentuated a sense of distinctiveness that verged again on the exotic.

Today, the "romanticism of the other" that has frequently marked the reception of Italian culture in America has not faded away. On the contrary, the myth of "Italian creativity" that has become widespread currency in many commercial sectors seems to have pervaded the way industrial design is, if not viewed, at least presented. But in an age where romantic images of Italy are used to publicize coffee shop franchises or condominiums in Florida, the risk of a trivialization of Italy's legacy in this important field of architectural culture need to be challenged. It is for this reason, among others, that a thorough analysis of how Italian industrial design has been viewed in the United States in the postwar years demands to be carried out with renewed urgency.

[1] Paul Valéry, "Orientem Versus," *Verve* 3 (October–December 1938), pp. 13–15; quoted from the 1962 English translation, *The Collected Works of Paul Valéry: History and Politics* (New York: Bollingen Foundation & Pantheon Books, 1962), p. 380.

[2] Ibid.

[3] Jane Schneider, "Introduction: The Dynamics of Neo-orientalism in Italy (1848–1995)," in Jane Schneider, ed., *Italy's "Southern Question": Orientalism in One Country* (Oxford and New York: Berg, 1998), pp. 1–23.

[4] Sponsored by the Compagnia Nazionale Artigiana and the Italian Ministry of Foreign Trade, the exhibition was primarily organized by Meyric Rogers, curator of Decorative Arts at the Art Institute of Chicago, and Charles Nagel, director of the Brooklyn Museum of Art.

[5] Meyric R. Rogers, *Italy at Work: Her Renaissance in Design Today* (Rome: Istituto Poligrafico dello Stato, 1950); cf. also Id., "Italy at Work: Her Renaissance in Design Today," *The Art Institute of Chicago Bulletin*, 45, 1 (February 1951), pp. 2–9; on the exhibition cf. also Rosalind Pepall, "Good Design is Good Business: Promoting Postwar Italian Design in America," in Giampiero Bosoni, ed., *Il Modo Italiano: Italian Design and Avant-garde in the 20th Century* (Milan and Montréal: Skira & The Montreal Museum of Fine Arts, 2006), pp. 68–79.

[6] Walter Dorwin Teague, "Foreword," in Rogers, *Italy at Work*, p. 9.

[7] Rogers, *Italy at Work*, p. 13.

[8] George E. Kidder Smith, *Italy Builds: Its Modern Architecture and Native Inheritance: Photographs by the Author* (London–New York–Milan: Architectural Press, Reinhold & Edizioni di Comunità, 1955); cf. also Id., "Native Italian Architecture. Contemporary Italian Architecture," typescript, American Association of Architectural Bibliographers, October 1954; Id., "The Modern Architecture of Italy," *Italian Quarterly*, 7–8 (1958–59), pp. 54–72. On Kidder Smith's book cf. Paolo Scrivano, "A Country Beyond Its Borders: Foreign Influences and Infiltrations in Postwar Italian Architecture," *2G* 15 (2000), pp. 12–17.

[9] Ernesto Nathan Rogers, "The Tradition of Modern Architecture in Italy," in Kidder Smith, *Italy Builds*, pp. 9–14.

[10] Kidder Smith, *Italy Builds*, p. 127.

[11] Francesco Tentori, "L'Italia Costruisce," *Architettura Cronache e Storia* 2, 7 (May 1956), p. 74.

[12] "Olivetti: Design in Industry," *The Museum of Modern Art Bulletin* 20, 1 (Fall 1952), p. 3 (special issue dedicated to the exhibition).

[13] "… there is nothing in the Olivetti showroom that provides so much as a hint of the singular combination of technical skills, productive efficiency, aesthetic taste, and social responsibility that makes this firm one of the most interesting industrial enterprises in the world": Lewis Mumford, "The Sky Line: Charivari and Confetti," *The New Yorker* (18 December 1954).

[14] "La nuova sede dell'Alitalia a New York," *Domus* 354 (May 1959), pp. 7–11.

[15] These data are quoted in Paul Ginsborg, *A History of Contemporary Italy: Society and Politics 1943–1988* (London: Penguin Books, 1990), p. 215.

[16] By 1967, for example, Italy was the third largest manufacturer of refrigerators in the world: Adriana Castagnoli and Emanuela Scarpellini, *Storia degli imprenditori italiani* (Turin: Einaudi, 2003), pp. 322–26.

[17] Emilio Ambasz (ed.), *Italy: The New Domestic Landscape: Achievements and Problems of Italian Design* (New York–Florence: The Museum of Modern Art & Centro Di, 1972).

*Nathalie Grenon**

Furnishing the Italian Chancery as a National Design Collection

* *Designer, Studio S.A.A., Rome*

We are particularly pleased with our success in creating unity between a modern building, the Italian Chancery in Washington, and the fixtures and furnishings that we either designed ourselves or selected from among the many examples of Italian excellence in the period from the 1950s to today.

From the individual offices to the meeting rooms, lounges, reception areas, and the auditorium, all the fixtures and furnishings characterizing the building's functional arrangement are unique pieces, selected with the criterion of creating a bona fide collection that will distinguish the Italian presence in Washington with a noteworthy element of design and establish a dialogue with the items from Italy on exhibit in New York at the MoMA.

We wish to review a few of the concepts that have distinguished our work on the Chancery. The Italian expression "*il buon design*" is not a neologism; we may find it in the writings of Leonardo da Vinci. It indicates a correspondence of the object with a rigorous ideal. It refers to a harmonious equilibrium among the different parts of a figurative or architectural work. It also expresses a way of conceiving life in civilized society where tradition and innovation are able to meet. When we bring together the efficiency of modern functional objects with the consummate perfection of their historical counterparts in a contraposition like that proposed by Baudrillard in *The System of Objects*, we are not solely seeking a harmonious relationship with the architectural space but also one with its ornamentation to affirm a recognizable model of life that bears the mark of individual creativity.

We did not choose to create our design collection from the latest products out of Milan's *Salone del Mobile*, but instead sought to construct a historical collection of Italian design between the end of the Second World War and the present day in order to represent the extraordinary versatility, productivity, and creativity of the now historicized objects found in major museum collections and other prestigious places. This work also stands without precedents among institutional buildings created by the Italian State in this period.

In achieving this, we had the complete collaboration of the major Italian design firms (Poltrona Frau, B&B, Fontana Arte, Flos, Artemide, and Unifor, to name just a few), who agreed to produce a number of historic pieces that are no longer in their catalogues, such as the *Luminator* lamp designed by Baldessari or the *Tangram* table conceived by Massimo Morozzi.

We thus achieved the dual objective of establishing a presence in the capital of the United States which effectively represents Italian excellence in design while also furthering the aspirations of the Italian firms to be represented in a prestigious institutional context.

As a counterpoint to the more contemporary objects, we recovered all the precious archaeological relics from the previous Chancery. Our work thus consisted of placing these extraordinary elements in key points in the new building.

Thanks to the design of their supports and the placement of these relics in significant places, visitors to encounter a magnificent Roman-epoch marble bust in the Ambassador's

The large carpet, design by Nathalie Grenon, made by Kasthall.
Left: *AEO* armchair, design by Archizoom, made by Cassina. *I feltri* armchair, design by Gaetano Pesce, made by Cassina.
Background: *Torso* sofa, design by Paolo Deganello, made by Cassina.
Right: *Interviste* seats, design by Vinelli Associati, made by Poltrona Frau.
Photo: Archivio S.A.A.

Large seats in the atrium, large elliptical sofa and *Diamond Big* armchairs, design by Nathalie Grenon for S.A.A., made by Poltrona Frau. Photo: Archivio S.A.A.

Black lacquered table, design by Carlo Scarpa, made by Gavina. Photo: Archivio S.A.A.

Modular *Quadrifoglio* table, design by Nathalie Grenon for S.A.A., made by Poltrona Frau. Photo: Archivio S.A.A.

Luminator lamp, design by Luciano Baldessari, made by Luce Plan. Photo: Archivio S.A.A.

entry hall, two large columns marking the main entrance, and a series of archaeological relics outlined against the greenery of the park.

We did respond to more than aesthetic criteria in our work, and the result is an arrangement that places objects of different stylistic extractions on the same critical level. Their heterogeneity exalts the qualities of each while delineating their trends, affinities and contrasts. Designer pieces, either single exemplars or serial productions, reveal the physiognomy of the Italian approach.

To get a better idea of what I am talking about, I would propose a visit to the Chancery, starting from the large central atrium giving access to all the visitor areas, including the auditorium.

The atrium is characterized by a Venetian mosaic floor made with fragments of the pink stone used on the facade laid out in a design that follows the perspective lines out into the park and to the horizon embellished by the Washington Monument. It is dominated by two spacious lounge areas characterized by curving sofas that we designed ad hoc for this space and by large *Diamond Big* armchairs, whose oversized stature engages in dialogue with the spaciousness of the atrium.

The meeting rooms, dining room and large salon all give onto the atrium. Each of these spaces has its own identity reinforced by its fixtures and furnishings.

There is a sort of "metaphysical" juxtaposition against the cobalt blue wall leading to the auditorium: on the left we have the black lacquered table designed by Carlo Scarpa for Gavina; on the right, an ancient white marble drapery.

In the meeting room we find a large central table designed for plenary sessions and a modular table system that can be adapted to a range of different needs. The basic module is a square table that can be made circular. It thus allows a variety of configurations for meetings or can be converted into independent 12-person tables for banquets. Large carpets made expressly for this location characterize the waiting areas, lounges and meeting areas in a progression from public to private space, from the atrium to the lounges to the second floor walkways that connect the two wings of the building.

Ala seats on the large carpet, design by Nathalie Grenon for S.A.A., made by Poltrona Frau. Archaeological relics against the windows onto the park.
Photo: Archivio S.A.A.

On the first carpet, which you find in the atrium, there are sofas and armchairs with exposed wooden frames that dialogue with the trees outdoors and accentuate the visual continuity with the wooded area outside the windows. These large carpets flow through the different spaces. The criterion used here was to create a central continuum within which the eclectic mix of design can merge and interact.

While in a museum convention would dictate a rather sterile arrangement of display objects, with one piece aligned with the next, in our case we are dealing with pieces that are actually used, and so we place them on these large carpets to contextualize their presence and specific function.

We developed a particular idea for the illumination. We sought to create a homey, welcoming tone with soft lighting that would characterize the general scene, against which a collection of floor, wall, and table lamps would stand out as bona fide sculptures of light that are beautiful whether on or off. The Italian approach to lamp design is characterized by a focus on the functional aspect but an even greater emphasis on the aesthetics, in order to transform the functional object into a beautiful sculpture.

We might extend this concept to the collection of bookcases marking out the circulation paths and waiting areas or complementing the desks in the offices.

They are all design pieces produced in limited or unlimited series with a great variety of formats. The only exception is the specially designed case for receiving and distributing diplomatic valises.

The large carpet, design by
Nathalie Grenon, made by Kasthall.
Table design by Carlo Scarpa, made
by Gavina. *Avio* chairs, design by
S.A.A., made by Poltrona Frau.
Photo: Archivio S.A.A.

Mail wall, design by S.A.A.
Photo: Alan Karchmher

Quadrifoglio table, design by
Nathalie Grenon for S.A.A., made
by Poltrona Frau. *Avio* chairs.
Right background: lounge with
seats, design by Vico Magistretti,
made by De Padova. *0024/s* lamps,
design by Gio Ponti, made by
Fontana Arte.
Left background: *Diamond Big*
armchairs, design by Nathalie
Grenon for S.A.A., made
by Poltrona Frau.
Photo: Alan Karchmher

Office of the Minister
Plenipotentiary.
Naos bookcase, design by Pierluigi
Cerri, made by Unifor. *Diamond*
armchairs, design by Nathalie
Grenon for S.A.A., made by Poltrona
Frau. Desk, design by S.A.A.
Photo: Alan Karchmher

Ambassador's private entrance.
Right: ancient cipollino marble column.
Velo ceiling lamp, design by Franco Raggi,
made by Fontana Arte.
Photo: Archivio S.A.A.

Entrance to Ambassador's office.
Ceramic, design by Ettore Sottsass, made
by Clair de Luna. Carpet, design by Nathalie
Grenon, made by Kasthall. *Oblio* lamp
and *Breck* chair, design by Pitero Beltrami,
made by Cassina.
Photo: Archivio S.A.A.

IN THIS TEMPLE
AS IN THE HEARTS OF THE PEOPLE
FOR WHOM HE SAVED THE UNION
THE MEMORY OF ABRAHAM LINCOLN
IS ENSHRINED FOREVER

*Ennio Caretto**

"Italian Imprints"

* *Journalist and correspondent,*
Corriere della Sera

As Washington prepared for the 1989 Columbus Day celebrations and the 200th anniversary of the U.S. Constitution, the *Washington Post* published an article titled "Italian Imprints," singing praises to the "sons of Italy." As historian Alan Kraut saw them, they were the ones who shaped the nation's capital, embodying in its monuments and institutions the nation's most sacred values, such as equality and democracy. Starting in the eighteenth century, Italian painters and sculptors, military men and politicians, architects and artisans, lawyers and teachers, masons and stone-cutters were welcomed or imported into Virginia and Maryland. They would later find purposeful work at the border between these two states, along the banks of the Potomac, on the site of the future Washington, D.C. This is a little-known chapter in the history of Italian emigration to the United States. It was a sort of Italian brain drain *ante litteram*, as opposed to the emigration of over two million laborers at the turn of the twentieth century. It was a chapter inscribed with the dream of the Founding Fathers to make Washington the new Rome.

Two other historians, Jerre Mangione and Ben Morreale, tell us that when he assembled the first military band, forerunner of the "President's own" Marine Band, Thomas Jefferson, the most "Italian" of the presidents, recruited 14 Italian musicians. They arrived in Washington in 1805 aboard the frigate *Chesapeake*, and quickly became the idols of the Washington elite, who were starved for music and concerts. In the capital, with its emerging federal buildings taking their inspiration from Rome, Italy was emblematized as the "mother of the arts." The elite studied Italian. In 1778, Jefferson, who read Italian, secured a professorship for Carlo Bellini, who had immigrated to the United States in 1774, at the College of William and Mary. Italian sculptors immortalized the Founding Fathers. Giuseppe Ceracchi, the most notable, who arrived in the capital in 1791, sculpted busts of George Washington, Thomas Jefferson, John Adams, James Madison, Benjamin Franklin, Alexander Hamilton, and others.

However, the deepest Italian imprint on the future Republic and its capital had been left some time earlier, and not by an artist, but by a surgeon, horticulturist, and political philosopher from Tuscany, Filippo Mazzei. Invited by Franklin and Adams, whom he had met in London, Mazzei had gone to Virginia with a small entourage with the assignment of making it a small agricultural paradise. He also made it a forge for liberty and democracy. His writings, signed with the pen name "Furioso," translated by his ally and mentor Jefferson and published in the *Virginia Gazette*, helped inspire the anticolonialist uprisings and he is reputed to have helped Jefferson in writing the *Declaration of Independence*, especially the composition of the phrase "all men are created equal." At the outbreak of the war against King George of England, Mazzei attempted to enlist in the army, but Jefferson prevented him, charging him instead with the task of collecting arms and funds in Europe, where he returned in 1785.

Between 1783, the year the British recognized American independence and the beginning of the American Republic, and 1871, the final year in Italy's unification process,

The statue of Abraham Lincoln sculpted by Attilio Piccirilli and his five brothers, based on a model by Daniel Chester French. Photo: Archivio Skira.

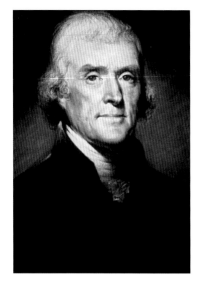

Rembrandt Peale, *Thomas Jefferson*, 1800.
© Bettmann Corbis, Milan.

no more than twelve thousand Italians settled in America, as opposed to a million and a half Germans and two million Irish. There were never more than a few hundred Italians in and around Washington. Mangione and Morreale cite the presence of Venetian artisans in Jamestown as early as 1621 and groups of textile workers in Maryland in 1649. They also state that the first Italian to receive U.S. citizenship, in 1784, was Francesco Vigo, an officer in the Spanish army who had made his fortune in the fur trade and later became a financier and secret agent for the Virginian general George Rogers Clark in the Revolutionary War. Vigo sacrificed his fortune to the cause and died in poverty with the rank of Colonel. In 1876, the American government awarded his heirs a life-annuity of fifty thousand dollars.

For over half of the nineteenth century, the Italianness of the Washington area was represented on the one hand by politicians and military men, and on the other by painters and sculptors. Outstanding among the former was Count Luigi Palma di Cesnola, one of the heroes of the Union army in the American Civil War. He was sent as American Consul to Cyprus by President Abraham Lincoln in 1865. An enthusiastic archaeologist, Cesnola came back from the island with such a collection of treasures that he was named director of the New York Metropolitan Museum. One of the notables among the painters and sculptors, Constantino Brumidi's monumental frescoes for the United States Capitol won him the nickname "Michelangelo of the United States." He arrived in the U.S. in 1852, a period of particular hostility towards immigrants, and for three years painted murals in the major churches of New York, Philadelphia, and Baltimore. Brumidi later moved to Washington, where he died accidentally in 1880 in a fall from a scaffolding.

The extraordinary love story between the capital and Italian artists unfolded in Brumidi's wake. In the subsequent half century, Attilio Piccirilli and his five brothers, whose studio was in New York, sculpted the statue of Lincoln on the Mall, based on drawings by Daniel Chester French. Andrea Bernasconi created the six statues on the facade of Union Station and the monument to Christopher Columbus. Gaetano Trentanove crafted

Detail of two of the six statues created by Andrea Bernasconi for the main facade of Union Station in Washington.
Photo: Archivio Skira.

David Jacques Louis, *Filippo Mazzei*.
Photo RMN © Daniel Arnaudet.

the statues of Albert Rike in Judiciary Square and Daniel Webster in Scott Circle. Various generations of Italian stone-cutters, the last of them being Vincenzo Palumbo from Molfetta at the close of the twentieth century, succeeded each other among the spires of the cathedral on the corner of Massachusetts and Wisconsin Avenue. Other arrivals from New York in the form of the first Italian operas, such as Rossini's *Barber of Seville*, began to reach Washington theaters.

In the early twentieth century, immigration to the U.S. capital changed face. The 1850 census recorded a mere 74 Italian nationals and there were still only 476 in 1890. But in 1910 their numbers had grown to 2,761, and now they were not just the brains but also the brawn. A cultural elite became intermixed with laborers, masons, barbers, farmers, and miners from West Virginia. The new arrivals found some of their predecessors in positions of power, from the grandchildren of Gaetano Carusi, director of the Marine Band in 1805, who had all become jurists and lawyers, to the children of Tullio Suzzara Verdi, who had become authorities in the medical field. The ones with the best backgrounds or the greatest luck followed in their footsteps, such as Nicola Reale, a violin maker, who gave one of his instruments to then Vice President Richard Nixon, a former violinist. But the majority of the Italians engaged in heavy labor, such as the construction of Union Station and the railways.

Washington was not an industrial city, it did not have its own Little Italy nor, fortunately, organized crime such as the Mano Nera or the Cosa Nostra. Unlike New York, where the Italian population exceeded 340,000, or Chicago, where there were more than 45,000, the small community of Italians in Washington lived scattered among the neighborhoods and suburbs. Two parallel phenomena took form: on the one hand, there were those who assimilated the American competitive spirit and emerged as figures of power, such as the builders Luigi Perna, Antonio Izzo, and Antonio Carrozza; on the other, associations were formed for the preservation of Italian culture, such as the Società Culturale Italiana and the Lido Civic Club, and later the Sons of Italy with their lodge. The first of them, the Società Culturale Italiana, founded in 1953 by Salvatore Castiglione, dates its origins back to the second half of the nineteenth century, when it donated a statue of Giuseppe Garibaldi to Congress. The bust, sculpted in 1888, was the work of Giuseppe Mantegnana, who had been commissioned by the Società to create a monument to Garibaldi, who had died six years earlier. He was the hero of the two worlds and the idol of Italians in America. In the Civil War, soldiers in both the Confederate and Union armies nicknamed the well-represented companies of Italian immigrants the "Garibaldi guards." The Union army formed them into the 39th Infantry Regiment of New York. Their banner was the same one used by Garibaldi in Lombardy in 1848 and in Rome in 1849. The Confederates assigned them to Sixth Regiment of the European Division. Prior to the Civil War, Garibaldi had spent two years on Staten Island with Antonio Meucci, working in a match factory. It is not known whether he visited Washington, but when the war broke out, he wrote to President Lincoln from abroad to offer his help in the conflict. Lincoln declined.

Since the 1920s, the main gathering place for Italians in Washington is father Nicola de Carlo's Church of the Holy Rosary. Don De Carlo, from Potenza, blessed the first stone laid in 1913, and presided from the First World War, through the Great Depression and the Second World War, into the early 1960s. The parish attracted the new arrivals from Italy, humble and capable, such as the food merchants Antonio and Mariano Litteri and the Catania family of bakers, who opened up shop respectively in 1926 and 1934, and like Alfonso Ciancio, who is reputed to have "asphalted half the streets in Georgetown." Father De Carlo, a formidable man with friends in Congress, protected his parishioners like a "benevolent godfather", as we read in an article published in the *Washingtonian Magazine*, finding work for them, providing assistance, and paying for their education.

Andrea Bernasconi, statue of Christopher
Columbus in front of Union Station.
Photo: Archivio Skira.

Interior of Saint Mark's church with frescoes
and principal mosaic by Italian artisans.
Photo: Archivio Skira.

It was a difficult mission. Between 1910 and 1930, another two million and a half Italians emigrated to the United States. They were too many and too late, too poor and too poorly educated, according to Mangione and Morreale. They soon became the objects of hostility and prejudice. Their image was sullied in the media with harsh denouncements of the "godfathers" who exploited them and stories about the Italian "bandits of the south." Even President Franklin Roosevelt scorned them. When the question arose as to whether to put them in internment camps after the United States declared war on Italy in 1941, he said, "I don't care so much about Italians, they are a lot of opera singers." (But in 1942, 600,000 Italians were classified "enemy aliens" and 3,300 were put into internment camps.) And so in Washington, as in the rest of the country, instead of a source of pride, being Italian was suddenly a source of shame or embarrassment: many Italians Americanized their names to ward off attention and took refuge in the suburbs. The Italian community would be rehabilitated by its active participation in the war effort.

It took Congress a half-century to apologize for the infamy of the internment camps, but Washington was generous with its "sons of Italy" who returned from the front and were organized into the Catholic Veterans by father De Carlo. The new generation of Italo-Americans could go to the university, as did the judge John Sirica, who in 1974, in the midst of the most serious political scandal in the history of the United States, would help bring down the Nixon presidency, and entrepreneurs like Dominic Antonelli the lord of the capital's parking lots (and buildings). It took about twenty years for Italianness to come back into favor, and this favor was especially strong in architecture. In a city half burned by the 1967 ghetto riots, the construction and urban renewal project for the Watergate complex was entrusted to Luigi Moretti. His project director, Giuseppe Cecchi, stayed in Washington, where he is now the "number one" builder and president of the Academy of Italian Cuisine.

The Church of the Holy Rosary, guided since 1962 by Don Cesare Donanzan, continued to make up for the lack of an Italian district. In the late 1980s, Donanzan founded the Casa Italiana next door to the church. Italian courses were given there, and weekly newspaper was published (its only predecessor being the Fascist magazine *Lo araldo*). It was also where the Villa Rosa festivals in Maryland were organized. The most popular Italian in the second half of the twentieth century in Washington, Pino Cicala, soon joined the community. Immediately after arriving from Sicily, Cicala opened an architecture studio in the Watergate complex with his brother Melo. However, his true calling was the media. For decades, starting in 1958, he directed a radio show, "Italian Melodies," and a television show, "Antenna Italia," which became the glue that held together the Italian community. Today, his website "Amico," which registers over 200,000 visits a month, represents an excellent guide to Italian Washington.

There is a long list of Italians who left a mark on the capital in the post-war period, ranging from Alessandro Crisafulli, professor of Romance literature at the Catholic University, Giorgio Tagliacozzo of the *Voice of America*, to the organist Riccardo Pellicano, who passed away in 2004 at the ripe old age of 101. One of the most important figures

GAYLORD LERUE GROZIER
LIEUTENANT COMMANDER
UNITED STATES NAVY
18 APR.1914 — 7 JULY 1973
HIS WIFE
SOPHIE MARIE GROZIER
5 FEB.1915 — 14 MAR.1961

GEORGE LOMAX
FIRST LIEUTENANT, 325
U.S. ARMY
BORN, ABBEVILLE
OCTOBER 8, 188
KILLED IN ARGONNE FORES
OCTOBER 17, 1918

LVIGI BARTOLVCCI DVNDAS
ITALIAN NAVY
1888-1920

Detail of the old Chancery of the Italian Embassy.
Photo: Archivio Skira.

Lisa Sergio, 1937.

was Lisa Sergio, daughter of a Tuscan baron and his American wife. She edited a weekly English newspaper in Florence called *Italian Mail*, which numbered D. H. Lawrence among its contributors. For five years she was the "golden voice" of Mussolini's foreign radio broadcasts. But her opposition to Fascism grew over time and she moved to New York in 1937. During the Second World War she was one of the most authoritative radio and television commentators. In later years, she would become the center of the Washington cultural circle. Another eminent Italian was Bruno Luzzatto, NATO advisor, who led the UN mission in Italy in 1948.

In the past thirty years, Washington brought the first Italo-Americans onto the political stage. These include President Johnson's spokesman, Jack Valenti, the minister of education, Joe Califano, the first woman to run for the vice presidency, Geraldine Ferraro, and President Clinton's chief of staff, John Podestà. But Italian distinction was mainly earned in the medical field. The forerunner of the world's foremost authorities on AIDS, Robert Gallo and Anthony Fauci, was Guilio Cantoni, Emeritus Scientist of the National Health Institute. Cantoni, a Milanese Jew who fled Fascism and found refuge in America thanks to the help of his dear friend Arturo Toscanini, served as founding chief of National Institute of Mental Health's intramural Laboratory of General and Comparative Biochemistry from 1954 to 1994, and as the founding music director of the FAES Chamber Music Series. A lover of music and translator of libretti, he invited the great Italian luminaries in the field of music, from Maurizio Pollini to the Virtuosi of Rome, to perform in the capital.

In a certain sense, in terms of its relationship with Italians, modern Washington has come full circle and returned to its historical roots. Today, like two centuries ago, Italy is a synonym for quality and art—the new Italian embassy attracts hordes of visitors—and immigration is represented by talent, not by labor, though this talent is prevalently in medicine and science rather than in the arts. The National Gallery of Art boasts one of the world's most extraordinary collections of Italian paintings, and Verdi and Puccini dominate at the Kennedy Center. And as all over America, Italian restaurants and boutiques are the most sought-after. In the register of Italians residing abroad (*Anagrafe degli Italiani Residenti all'Estero* – AIRE), there are some four thousand recorded as residing in Washington, but not everyone registers. The Italo-Americans in the area around the nation's capital exceed six hundred thousand, and the Sons of Italy have been joined in their representation of Italian immigrants by the National Italian American Foundation (NIAF).

The motto of the Founding Fathers who sought to reproduce ancient Rome along the banks of the Potomac, "Italy is near," reverberates in public places as well as in the salons of high society, and is emphasized by the homage the city has paid to great Italians: Volta Street, the only Georgetown street dedicated to a historic figure; the bronze bust of Dante, sculpted by Ettore Ximenes for the poet's 600th birthday; the monument to fallen Italians in Arlington Cemetery; the statue of the Jesuit Eusebio Chino, who explored the Spanish empire in North America, the "far west," around the turn of the eighteenth century.

Italy is near, but no longer just on the level of culture and ideals, but also for its contribution to the city's physical development. The eagle symbolizes the United States of America, and it is no coincidence that the stone-cutter known in the first half of the twentieth century as "Washington eagle man" was Giorgio Giannetti: an Italian.

179

The main facade of the Holy Rosary Church.

The nave and the altar.

pp. 182–83
Details of the statuary decorations
on the Casa Italiana.

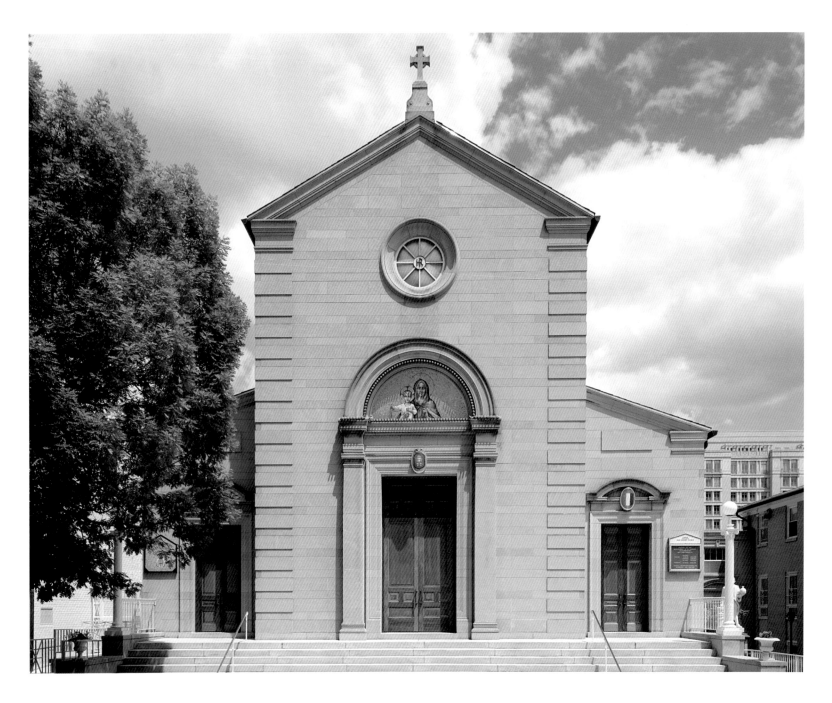

The church has been at the heart of the religious life of the Italian community in Washington since the early 1900s when the archbishop Giovanni Bonzano, Apostolic delegate to the United States, summoned the very young priest, father Nicola De Carlo, to organize the Italian-speaking Catholics in the city. Today's church is the fruit of the efforts of father Nicola and the community of artisans and workers who gave concrete form to a locus for the spiritual life of the community. The Holy Rosary Church was designed by the Roman architect Aristide Leonori (who had previously conceived the Catholic cathedrals in St. Louis, Missouri and Buffalo, New York) in keeping with the characteristics of early Italian Renaissance churches. The facade and exterior walls are faced in granite, while the interiors are finished in stucco and *scagliola* with decorations and stained glass windows crafted by immigrant Italian artisans. In spite of the First World War, construction began in 1918 and was completed with a grand public ceremony in 1923. In the ensuing years, father De Carlo had an auditorium built and a bell tower was added in 1947. In the 1970s, under the supervision of the new pastor, father Caesar Donanzan, work began on what would become the Casa Italiana in 1983, a neo-Renaissance building that is a perfect complement to the church.

Details of the stained glass windows
in the Holy Rosary Church.

pp. 186–87
Details of an aisle and church ornaments.

DONATA DALLA CONFRATERNITA DI S. GABRIELE.

H. F. Huber
and Russell O. Kluge
Villa Firenze
Washington

1927

Villa Firenze viewed from the inner yard.

Villa Firenze, the Residence of the Italian Ambassador in the District of Columbia, is located in the large Rock Creek Park residential area.

Designed by the architects H. F. Huber and Russell O. Kluge in Tudor style for Blanche Estabrook, descended from an important family of builders, and completed in 1927, this impressive 21,370 square foot villa set on 22 acres of land with over 10,000 trees is one of the finest diplomatic residences for environmental setting and architectural quality.

The villa passed through a number of hands before becoming property of the Republic of Italy in 1976. From 1930 until 1941 it was leased to the Hungarian Embassy. It was then purchased by Colonel Robert Guggenheim, who named it after his mother, Florence. After being damaged by fire in 1946, the villa was restored by the architect Michael Rosenauer.

The entire ground floor is dedicated to entertainment functions. It contains a spacious entrance hall three stories high, a grand salon for receiving guests and a large dining room. One of the singular characteristics of this floor is the small rotunda situated between the hall and the grand salon. The bookcase in the study to the left of the entrance is an exact replica of one found in the study of the British architect Sir Christopher Wren in Oxford.

Since acquiring the villa, Italy has limited work on it to needed technical improvements while dedicating constant and ongoing attention to the careful restoration and protection of its wealth of art and craftsmanship.

James Earle Fraser
Equestrian Statues
Washington
1948–1951

One of the two pairs of statues.
Photo: Archivio Skira.

James E. Fraser in his studio with the completed plaster model.

Casting of Music and Harvest.

Crating statues for shipment to Italy.

Installation of the statues.

Unveiling of the statues and dedication.

The four bronze statues symbolizing Aspiration, Literature, Music, and the Harvest created by the American sculptor James Earle Fraser, and the two symbolizing Sacrifice and Valor by Leo Friedlander were a gift from Italy to seal the bond of friendship between the two peoples after the trauma of the Second World War.

The impressive statues flank the entrance to the Rock Creek Parkway behind the Lincoln Memorial. They were conceived and created in the late 1940s by Fraser, cast in Italy and unveiled in a grand public ceremony in West Potomac Park in the summer of 1951.

Harvest, Literature (*left*)
Valor, by Leo Friedlander (*right*)
Photos: Archivio Skira.